KICKED OUT OF THE GARDEN

Kimberly Ruth Taylor's book is a journey of strength, courage, and truth. Her words come from the heart, and her wisdom speaks to a life of fearlessly following God and her calling. *Kicked out of the Garden* will give you a new perspective on what it means to dream. Love flows from these pages and it will change you.

Jesse Blair, singer, songwriter

If you desire to be free from the rules and confusion of man-made religion and would like the freedom to make choices in your life with the Bible as a metaphor and Christ as a true friend, read this book!

Kimberly Ruth Taylor is a woman who has the courage and wisdom to save her Heart, her Spirit and her Family from being victims of fallen beliefs. Her trust in Jesus has given her the strength to step out of fear into a life that God wants for all of us!

John H. Clark, cowboy, faith songwriter

As one of the editors of this book, I had the benefit of becoming totally immersed in its essence and message. As each chapter unfolded I began to notice that I wasn't just reorganizing the material but the material was reorganizing me. Specifically it began to clarify my understanding of my own heart and the importance of learning to trust its power and presence, and how the most important thing we can do for ourselves and the planet today is to refuse to step into duality. Also as someone who was raised in the Christian faith under the tutelage of a very punitive vicar in the north of England, I was able to reframe a great deal of that negative experience and emerge with a deeper under-standing of Jesus and a more loving relationship with God. I highly recommend this book for anyone who is sincere about following the path of their heart whether you are religious or not. **Elaine Alghani**, writer, shamanic artist, healer and "entrepreneur"

Kimberly Ruth Taylor's writings, I must admit, are very mind opening and soul searching. Her book has allowed me to take my Christian faith out of the human box made by the laws of the church created by man. Her book is very spiritually and mind provoking. It is a very deep book that should not be read quickly. Like a fine wine, it needs to be slowly sipped and savored, grasping the message that only God can bestow upon you.
Beth Callahan, mother, friend, publisher, editor, and elected official

Kicked out of the Garden

Embracing Diversity as a Way of the Heart

Kicked out of the Garden

Embracing Diversity as a Way of the Heart

Kimberly Ruth Taylor

CHANGE
MAKERS
BOOKS

Winchester, UK
Washington, USA

First published by Changemakers Books, 2013
Changemakers Books is an imprint of John Hunt Publishing Ltd., Laurel House, Station Approach,
Alresford, Hants, SO24 9JH, UK
office1@jhpbooks.net
www.johnhuntpublishing.com
www.changemakers-books.com

For distributor details and how to order please visit the 'Ordering' section on our website.

Text copyright: Kimberly Ruth Taylor 2012

ISBN: 978 1 78099 990 6

A CIP catalogue record for this book is available from the British Library.

Design: Stuart Davies
Illustrations: Judy Delseno

Printed in the USA by Edwards Brothers Malloy

We operate a distinctive and ethical publishing philosophy in all
areas of our business, from our global network of authors to
production and worldwide distribution.

CONTENTS

I dedicate this book to Love, love of the Divine Creator of all there is, love of each other, and love of self.

Preface

My reason for writing this book was simple: I wanted to share my journey from a life of religious duality to a life of freedom and love. I hope that the revelations I received along the way might encourage others who have felt trapped or confused by their own spiritual belief systems, and those who have suffered from depression and the feeling of being "less than." Since I have been freed from the prison of religious dogma and learned to see the teachings of the Bible as metaphors rather than rules, I have come to know that it is possible to have a unique relationship with God through the portal of your own heart. By sharing my own truth, struggles, and triumphs, I hope to inspire you to step back into the garden of your heart and find renewed faith, freedom, and inner peace.

When I stepped off the path I was raised to walk—the path my family so diligently followed—I found myself stepping into the great unknown. This brought up many questions about the God that I had grown up with. Questions like, "What does He really require of me?" and "What do I need to do to step out of fear and into life and abundance?" As I became more comfortable with my journey, I began to see all of the illusions that created my fears, and came to understood that God would find me if I ever got lost.

So far, this journey has brought me much life and great joy. The joy I'm experiencing now came as I allowed myself to feel and release my limiting spiritual beliefs, fears, and sorrows. Today I can say wholeheartedly that God is good and I am grateful to be alive!

So here is the story of my healing. I am honored to share it with you, and I hope that it makes as much of a difference in your life as it has in mine.

I wish you many blessings on your heart path.

Kimberly Ruth Taylor

Chapter 1

In the Beginning

When I was 9, my parents sent me away to church camp. It was my first time away from home. It was also where I first heard that Jesus had a message especially for me. I was told that he had come to earth to show me who God was, and how God saw and felt about me. This got my full attention, and from that moment on I was dedicated to discovering more about this great mystery. I looked forward to going to church with my family each week, and as I learned more about the teachings of Christ, I fell in love with this great being.

I was also told how I was supposed to act in order to have a relationship with the God of all Gods.

I tried very hard to become all that I was told God wanted me to be. It was important to me that I pleased Him in the "proper" manner. This led to many years of trying and pleasing, which put me further and further away from my own heart and voice.

In church I was told that the only way to know God was by accepting Jesus as my personal savior. I didn't know what this meant, but because I so dearly wanted to know God, I pretended to understand and I acted as if I did know. I was afraid that if I voiced any difficulty, I would be rejected from the fold of believers. And yet I could never make sense of it; something was always missing. Accepting Jesus fully and completely was the foundation of my faith, and yet I couldn't feel the depth of this critical piece. I began to think that there was something wrong with me because of this.

What I did know was how I felt about Jesus, and how his presence affected my life. He gave me great strength in difficult times, and I could sense his love for me. I didn't have the same sense about God though. I didn't feel worthy of God's love. Even when I could feel how much God loved others, I couldn't feel it for myself. I was told that the reason Jesus came to earth was so I could see how much God loved me, and yet I just couldn't fathom it.

By the time I got to college, I had decided to become a missionary. I thought that helping others find God would help me find the piece that was missing for me, the one that would connect me to the Great I AM presence. I was certain it would fill the void inside of me that caused me such great despair.

I began to strictly follow all the rules of the church. I was told that if I lived this way, I would be a viable asset to God. In spite of these efforts, I eventually realized that I was just like the whitewashed tombs that Jesus spoke of: I was all clean and nicely painted on the outside, but on the inside there was decaying flesh.

Outwardly I was following all the rules; inwardly I felt unacceptable because of the way I was thinking and feeling. I believed that the thoughts and emotions I had were not what a good Christian woman who loves God should think and feel. But the more I tried to control them, the heavier my life became and the stronger my depression. I hated that depression. I tried everything I could to get away from it, only to find that the more I ran, the more powerful a hold it had on my life.

"What's wrong with me?" I asked myself. I had no apparent reason to be depressed. My life was full and I had a loving family. I enjoyed my friends and I was cared for in every way, and yet this cloud of depression just kept getting bigger.

By then I was well into college and decided to change my major from missions to art education, which took me to a state school in Ohio close to my family. I realized that I was most gifted in art and creativity, and although I still wanted to help people find God, the missionary curriculum was just too dry. I was also starting to question all of the beliefs I had held.

During this time, a friend had a serious hiking accident that put him in a semi-comatose state. I was very upset by this and wanted so much to help him. I remembered the story in the Bible about faith the size of a mustard seed being able to move a mountain. So I began to pray diligently for his full recovery. I tried so hard to be that mustard seed, but no matter how hard I prayed, my friend didn't recover.

To me, this proved once again that I wasn't good enough. My insides didn't match who I appeared to be on the outside. I realized I only believed what I believed because it was what I had been taught by my parents and the church. I had never openly questioned these teachings or considered that there might be another way to feel God's love and presence in my heart. I continued to address the emptiness I felt by trying to do more of what I thought was expected of me—what I had been told would please God. But I felt worthless and faithless and couldn't imagine how the God of Gods could find any favor in me whatsoever.

As time passed, I was ready to forsake all of the beliefs I had grown up with. Except for Jesus, for it was only through him that I felt any kind of connection to God. Even then, I still didn't know how to separate him from all the rules I had learned growing up. I believed that if I stepped away from God, I had to step away from Jesus, too. I soon came to the painful understanding that I had no faith and very little love.

It wasn't until I noticed how limited my love was for others that I began to sense the difference between me and the Christ I loved and tried to emulate. His love was unconditional. My love was conditional. I felt that the people in my life had to believe and speak as I did in order for me to accept them. I had so many judgments about others, and judgment definitely wasn't what Jesus came to show us. I lived my life feeling less than the person I actually was. I never felt I was enough.

The problem is that when you feel that you are never enough, you spend all of your time trying to justify your existence. And if you live your life trying to justify your existence, the hole inside of you gets bigger and emptier. You try harder and harder, only to feel less and less worthy. I was trapped in a vicious circle of unworthiness. Jesus always spoke about freedom and love and how our cups would overflow with the beautiful fruit of the spirit. Yet I only felt limitation and shame for what I was not. I had no idea how to connect with the abundance and life that Jesus described. The rules I had always attempted to follow left no room for passion or joy.

When I was young, I prayed to God to free me from my

passion because I felt passion would lead me to being out of control. I now know that passion is one of the greatest guides to an open heart. It was the lack of passion in my life that made it hard for me to live freely and joyfully. Since then, my prayer has changed to, "Great Mystery, free me to live my passion."

Passion springs from the soul and sings the song that removes any obstacles that prevent our heart from opening. It allows the heart to lead us on our journey. And when the heart is leading, our dance becomes flowing and graceful. Our journey is filled with the joy, freedom, and beauty we never realized was there to be received. I believe that this is the reason Jesus came to earth and embodied the essence of the Great Divine. He came to show us the way back to ourselves and to our true passion for life.

So many of us are unable to step back into the garden of our heart because we've separated from our own soul. This is what leads to feelings of guilt, shame, and unworthiness, and ultimately causes us to lose our heart connection. I tried to bridge that gap in myself by doing mighty and loving works, only to find myself worn out, depressed, and discouraged. My life felt like a boulder I was pushing uphill. I see this in others' lives too. The more we push, the further we get from our heart and its calling. And when we are not fully present in our heart, we can't live up to the standards that we set for ourselves. We are blind to the image of God that is reflected in us and can only perceive what we lack.

When we cut ourselves off from the living waters of our heart, the fruit of our soul cannot help but get old, dry, and bitter from lack of sweetness. I saw this happen to my mother, and couldn't let the same thing happen to me or my own children. So I joined forces with my heart, stepped out in new ways, and watched as my life and the lives of those closest to me transformed.

Now I no longer struggle with depression. I live my life to the fullest, and I'm committed to allowing the truth in my heart to be my compass. Although this led me to leave my marriage of 28 years, it has also been the gateway to many miracles. When I left, I told God that I would only follow my heart if He promised to take care of my husband and my seven children. This He has done beyond my wildest dreams.

Chapter 2

My Beloved Mother

The person who prompted me to begin my healing journey was my beloved mother, Erika Elsa Zendel, who left this world in December of 2009. As a young girl I was awed by her beauty and spirituality. She was an amazing beacon of light.

My mother was born in 1934. Her parents were German immigrants who met in America. My grandmother came over by herself in search of greater opportunity. My grandfather came over to repay a family that had sent his family money, food, and supplies during the First World War. The supplies this family sent allowed my grandfather's family to keep their welding business going when many other businesses were not able to survive the war. Because of this, my great grandmother decreed that one of her six children had to go work for this family to thank them for all they did. At that point, my grandfather was the only son who didn't have a family of his own, so they felt he would be the best choice.

My mother was the only child to grace my grandparents' life, so all the focus was on her. My grandmother was very controlling and protective and made all the decisions for my mother. She decided what my mother would wear to school every day, all the way up through high school; she also decided where my mother would go to college and what she would major in. My mother wanted to go to Miami University in Oxford, Ohio, and major in business, but my grandmother decided that she would go to the Conservatory of Music in Cincinnati, Ohio, and major in voice. This lack of freedom left a very strong mark on my mother.

My mother was a deeply spiritual woman. When she was young, many people flocked to her door for teaching and spiritual advice. She was very organized and people enjoyed following her. She always assumed leadership positions in whatever area she chose to focus on. The majority of her focus was on the church. My dad, on the other hand, "never met a stranger," but wasn't able to step into the deeper realms of conversation with people. He always thought everyone was coming to see him, but in reality, it was my mother that drew people in.

As my mom aged, fewer and fewer people came to her door for advice and teaching. Her beautiful light seemed to get dimmer and dimmer. What seemed to be putting it out was her anger. She was angry at her family, and especially angry at my dad. I believe my dad was a very needy man, and that my mom had let him feed off her their entire married life. He had low self-esteem and always looked to her to tell him he was alright and that his choices were good. My dad constantly wanted building up and my mom thought it was her role in life to do so. It seems like my dad always did what he wanted to do. And if that wasn't working, my mom would scramble to make it right. Whether the issue was raising three children or managing the finances, my mother was always the one responsible for making life work.

My mom never allowed herself to do what she wanted to do. She always did what others wanted her to do, and this took a heavy toll on her soul. In the end, it left her with little ability to show love. As she got older, she was constantly frustrated. I watched as the fruits of her spirit—love, joy, peace, patience, and kindness—rotted away. Instead she became bitter, angry, and afraid.

This change in my mother has always plagued me. How could this happen to a woman that loved God and other people as much as she did? She was such a beautiful beacon of love and light in her younger years. What happened to the beautiful life of grace and joy that God promises those that love Him? The most certain thing in my mom's life was her love of the Divine, and she pursued this love with a vengeance. So how did her life become so limited and full of anger? I had to find the answer to this question because I saw so many parallels between her life and my own. Was I going to end up as unhappy as she was? Was there anything I could do to change that for myself?

Witnessing this sad transformation made me afraid to grow old. I had seven children of my own and I didn't want to pass on a legacy of fear. As a result, I began to ask myself what had gone so very wrong to allow someone as beautiful as my mother to change so drastically. The answers helped me find the courage to step out of my comfort zone and into my healing journey.

As I looked back on my mother's life, I saw that her great desire to know God and her love of humanity created a life filled with much responsibility. This responsibility seemed to deplete her light and her gifts more and more as time went by. She started to resent all that was being asked of her, whether it be by the church or family or friends. Her passion for life slowly disappeared as she became more controlled by the external world and its needs. For her, everyone else came first, and she made herself available to whomever she felt was most in need at the time. "Most in need" could never be her, and so she lived her life in a continual double bind. My mother's desire to serve, combined with her inability to listen to her heart, provided her with few options for true love and freedom. There was no room for her to follow her heart or her passion.

I remember the two of us sitting at the kitchen table, having what I thought was a wonderful time making flower arrangements. But she was unable to allow herself to relax and enjoy the moment, choosing instead to talk about all of the things she should have been doing. And so the opportunity to take pleasure in doing something she loved with her daughter passed her by. Another time, she shared with me that out of all the fruits of the spirit, it was the fruit of contentment that she could never get close to finding.

To be truly content, our heart and our actions have to be in alignment. We have to be completely present in the moment. Whenever we leave the heart out of the equation, contentment will elude us. And until we are content with what is, we can never really know what it means to die to the self and be free to follow our heart path. To be content means our insides and our outsides are congruent. This allows us to be free to be ourselves and let go of the parts of us that no longer serve us; the parts that prevent us from finding our soul.

For me, dying to self means stepping out of my head and into my heart, or out of the literal and into the metaphorical. The head only enslaves us with words like "should," "must," "try," and "obligation." The head possesses no magic.

By the "self," I mean the voices that come from my head. Some people call it the "small self" or the "negative ego." These voices tell us to try harder, and drive so many of our actions with fear, guilt, and shame. These are the voices that distract us, telling us that we don't make the cut before God and that what we want doesn't matter. They are the voices of the "shoulds." It was these voices that enslaved both my mother and me into doing good works. We both believed that they were coming from God. We had been taught that God's wants were non-negotiable, written in stone, and had nothing in common with our own wants.

I now believe these voices try to fill the void created by our desire to be closer to God, but only cause misery and insecurity. They tell us to do more and more to fill the bottomless pit of our unworthiness, and rob us of the life of abundance God has waiting for us if we will just allow it. The way to allow it is to begin to live life through the heart, which means listening to our heart and honoring it.

My mother wasn't able to see the connection between listening to her heart and knowing God. For many years, I was under the same illusion she was: the illusion that diligent service and sacrificing the desires of the heart would bring us closer to the Divine. Fortunately, I have found that if I want to experience the great abundance that God promises, I have to step out of my head and into my heart. I can't find it externally by doing good works, hearing the right speakers, or filling my head with knowledge about the Great I AM.

As I stepped into my heart, the voices telling me I was not enough got quieter. I came to understand that they were not of God, because they were driven by everything that is not love. God is love; therefore the voices of negativity cannot be of God.

Once I realized this, the voices no longer controlled me. I could hear my heart more clearly and I began to die to self. When I dropped into my heart, I found that I could hear the voice of my soul, which was the "still small voice" inside of me. This voice has given me the direction I needed for my life to flourish. I spent so much of my life in search of this, and I am very grateful to be able to say now, with sincerity, that it's good to be alive and it's good to be me.

It is in the heart where life steps out of the literal and into the metaphorical. This is where the power of creation resides, and where we can be most like God Himself. The Divine exists in our hearts. The map to our soul and our soul's calling can only be accessed through the whispers of our own heart song. The more I am able to drop into this space, the more my existence is filled with all the abundance life has to offer. I am able to reap the fruit of my vine and freely offer my gifts to the world and my family from a heart-centered place. And none of these offerings cost me anything because they flow so freely from within me.

Love and Fear

We cannot look to logic to find comfort, as true comfort and safety come from within. Life will never go exactly as we plan, and the literal, logical world can only meet our expectations for fleeting moments at best. Living only from the head makes it very difficult to determine our soul map and our calling, because all of the choices we make from that place are based on our need for external safety. A saying I love states, "Fear and anger say, 'Come with me; I will make you safe.' Love and acceptance say, 'Come with me; you are safe.'"

Our outer world is always changing, so earthly logic has no resting place in it. Love and acceptance are created when we can see and feel God through our heart. His love and the safety and comfort it affords us are not contingent on anything outside of ourselves. He is unchanging and infinite and His love is always present in our hearts. So even if we were to lose everything externally, we can remain safe within because God is always with us.

Feelings of fear and anger usually indicate that we are looking for security and safety in the external world. As my mother got older, she seemed to depend more on fear and anger to control her world and the people in it. I believe that she didn't feel safe, and was screaming out in anger because she wasn't able to listen to her heart or honor its voice. Although I'm saddened that she couldn't give herself the beauty that connecting with her soul would have brought, I honor her for all the beauty that she brought into my life and the example that she was to me. She showed me very clearly that I needed to step out and begin to search for myself. Even though my mother has passed on, I believe the greatest gift I ever gave her was embarking on my own search for freedom.

At first I was afraid to step out on this journey because I thought it might cause me to turn away from the God I had spent my whole life coming to know and serve. Many of the stories told to me when I was growing up were about people who had taken another path, lost their way, and turned away from the Great I AM. These stories all came rushing back to me, creating fear, until I remembered that fear is not of God. Fear only limits what we allow to come to us from God.

So in spite of my apprehension, I stepped away from my old familiar path and onto a new one. I began to look at other religions and what they believed, and opened myself up to other perspectives on the Great I AM. I allowed myself to work with a healer that was not a "born-again believer." I was in awe of her connection to Spirit, as she called God, and was very grateful for her teachings. She gave me much-needed freedom from my guilt and shame.

This new path felt uncomfortable at first, as it forced me to review many of my old beliefs: beliefs that had once made me feel very safe, yet limited my freedom and my heart. But it's normal to feel uncomfortable when making great changes, and I wasn't going to let discomfort be a reason to avoid my quest. I needed to continue on for my mother, my children, and myself. I was being called by my heart to venture far off the path my mother had so diligently followed. I was afraid of getting lost and losing the God I loved so much. And yet my mother had lost her way while holding tightly to all she had been taught.

At that time, I found comfort, guidance, and inspiration in the

Biblical parable of the lost sheep. In this parable, a shepherd was putting his sheep into the fold one night when he noticed that one was missing. Once he had the rest of the flock secured, he went to look for that one lost sheep and didn't come back until it was found. I realized I was that lost sheep. As I allowed the metaphor of this story to unfold, I saw that I had spent my life in the field with God. He knew me absolutely, like the shepherd knew his flock, and I knew He would keep me safe. We love each other, and He is concerned with all aspects of my well-being. This good shepherd wants the best for me. He wants to give me all the beauty life has to offer.

God spoke to me through this parable, showing me it is safe to step out and to go on every trail I desire without worrying about getting lost. If I go too far, my good shepherd promises to find me and bring me back to safety. By stepping into my fears and knowing God is with me no matter what, I find freedom from my limiting mind's control. And when I drop into my heart's truth and love, I see that fear is just an illusion that I can choose to let go of. Once I am free of fear, I can see that all things are possible through God, and I can receive all the power and miracles that He has in store for me.

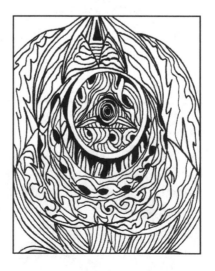

Chapter 3

Coming Home to the Garden

Looking back, it was in the early days of raising my children that my relationship to "doing" in order to justify my existence to God began to change. I had married young and stepped into motherhood a few years later. Raising a family was hard work and much of my time was spent at home with my little ones. I cherished the evenings when my husband came home from work. Within the first six years of my marriage I had four children. By the time I had been married 22 years, I had seven. My children gave me great purpose in life, as well as great feelings of love. They also helped strip me of all the activities I did to justify my life before myself and God. I learned so many lessons during that period in my life; lessons that changed how I saw God and helped me form the relationship I have with Him now.

My husband and I loved to put the kids to bed early and spend the rest of the evening talking about what was most prevalent in our hearts. For me, that was the struggle I had with myself and not feeling I was enough before God. At that time, I had my husband's constant support and assurance that I was enough just as I was. I felt those words deep in my soul and clung to them like a life raft because I was getting more depressed.

When I was young, depression only showed up when times were hard, but as I got older it never seemed to go away. I felt depressed whether it was a good day or a bad day; it was like a filter that limited the flow of beauty and energy into my life. I learned that guilt was a significant factor in creating my depression, so I took a big risk and stepped away from the church for a time. Being involved in the church and its teachings only seemed to exaggerate my guilt, and when I felt guilty I couldn't see anything for what it truly was.

This is when I learned to appreciate and celebrate spiritual diversity, and came to understand that diversity in all things is essential to life and God's plan. Away from the church and its rules about right and wrong, I was able to form deep spiritual connections with people who would have been considered backsliders and nonbelievers in the evangelical system I grew up in. These relationships made me feel closer to God than I had ever felt before. It was a magical time. I felt seen, loved, embraced, and supported. The women who I felt such acceptance from and connection to were teaching me to take care of myself in ways that my mother and the church hadn't been able to. They showed me that it was time to fill my cup so I could give to others from a fuller place.

And yet my depression persisted. At this point I had six young beings and a husband to take care of and I was running a busy household. Depression was becoming a daily struggle and I felt like it would never leave. I had received many blessings throughout my life and many of my prayers had been answered. I was surrounded by love in all of my relationships. Logically it made no sense, and I felt guilty about it. Judging myself fed the depression all the more. I was trapped in a vicious circle. Being a mother was my greatest calling, yet I thought I was messing it up big time. I couldn't shake the feeling that I came up short of what I should be as a mother. I couldn't escape my own guilt and judgment; I could only see what I was not. Even though I had left the church, the church was still very much in me.

Then my husband was offered a new business opportunity and we decided to move. The move was very hard on me because I had come to depend on my friends more than my husband for support. He had become more and more lifeless, spending much of his time at home alone in front of the TV with a drink. I was concerned that if he stayed in his present job it would kill him, as he had shared some alarming dreams on the subject. Sadly, I left the magical place where I had found so much support and moved closer to my family of origin.

The move put me into an even deeper state of depression. Even though I made friends in the new place, I didn't feel as supported as I had in the other community. My children were getting older and becoming more complicated to raise. I was feeling more hopeless and lifeless, and because of that had to stop doing many outside activities. It was everything I could do to keep that dark cloud from overtaking me and impacting my children's lives. I was exhausted, and my depression left me with little joy and no hope.

When you have little joy and no hope you become very moody. After watching my mom grow old and lose all her joy, I tried very hard to hide my negative feelings from my kids. By then I knew that my negativity came from a deep fear of aging and becoming like my mother. I wanted so much to give my children different options. I wanted them to know that they could age with grace and beauty and enjoy all the fruits of their life. So when my oldest son came home from college for spring break his sophomore year, drowning under his own cloud of depression, it struck a very deep chord in me.

This son has always been a mirror for me; I see so much of me in him. When he looked at me that day and said, "I don't believe in change," it touched me profoundly. I could sense his soul was dying. At 19, he was saying something that I had only come to feel at 40, and I knew he wasn't going to make it to 40 if he already felt this way. In addition, he had three important friends who had experienced family members committing suicide. This told me I had better do something to change, and do it fast because my son's life was at stake.

So at a very deep level, I vowed to find an answer. It came through one of my closest friends, who lived in the magical place where I had found so much support and solace. She called me around that time, and asked if I would want to do a workshop with her. She laughed and said, "There's a class I want you to take with me. It's about birth imprints, and I think it is going to change your life."

I entered the class feeling guilty and ashamed of never living up to what I wanted to be before my family and God. When the instructor asked us to say a little bit about ourselves, I remember welling up with tears and saying I was afraid the class would reveal more things for me to feel guilty about regarding how I had birthed and raised my kids. I didn't think I could take any more guilt, as it was already destroying me and my beauty.

Thankfully the experience did quite the opposite. It began to free me of the guilt that had seeped into every area of my life and was sucking me dry. The class gave me many insights into why I felt the way I did and some very powerful emotional releases. I was able to let go of many negative feelings I had been holding within me. This in turn loosened the hold that my depression had over me. I also discovered that the more I recognized my own beauty, the smaller my cloud of depression became. I took the first small steps toward falling in love with myself.

This love affair with myself was so exhilarating and freeing that I began to see that my struggle was not about God's love and forgiveness of me, but about my love and forgiveness of myself. My own self-judgment and separation from my heart had been killing my spirit and burying my life. God had always loved and forgiven me; I had abandoned myself by choosing to eat the fruit of judgment and duality. I had been living in the polarity of right versus wrong, whereas God had always seen me as perfect. All my limitations were coming from me. I couldn't dwell in the Garden where all life flows until I was able to let go of my internal separation.

After that, many things came to aid my healing. I came to understand that the greatest thing I could do for the well-being of my family was to step into my healing and embrace myself. I began by acknowledging to myself what I wanted, and even though I wasn't able to acknowledge it to others at that point, it was a start. As I did this, I was better able to let my desires be known and gained the courage to pursue them. This powerful process began freeing me from the grip of depression more and more.

I learned that if our belief system depends upon justifying our self through duality, then life will never feel full. Justification depends on comparison, and when we compare, we eat from the Tree of the Knowledge of Good and Evil instead of the Tree of Life. We need duality to some degree in order to master our life experiences: in order to understand hot, we need to experience cold, and to understand joy, we need to feel sadness. But living too much from duality causes great suffering.

Many forms of Christianity create duality by insisting that we interpret the Bible literally rather than encouraging us to find our own metaphors in its beautiful stories and teachings. Each sect interprets the Bible differently, and each insists that its version is the one true word of the Divine. This creates more and more rules, out of which more separation is born, even within communities of people who share the same faith.

Many people are afraid that if they look at the Bible metaphorically, it will take away its truth. But if they were willing to do this, they would find fear and separation melting away as they found their own truth in the word of God. We don't need to be afraid that our heart will steer us in the wrong direction, for God is in our heart. Personal metaphor is most like the Creator because it is endless in its teachings, just as the Divine is endless. By interpreting the Bible through my heart, I have finally begun to understand what Christ represents in the Divine scheme of life.

If you take the story of the Garden of Eden, for instance, it doesn't really matter whether it happened in physical form or not. It exists just as powerfully as a metaphor. For me, this story functions as a guiding light, supporting my journey out of duality and into freedom from separation and depression.

I believe the essence of the story is God's relationship with us and the importance of choice. God didn't order Adam and Eve not to eat from the Tree of Knowledge of Good and Evil; he said that it would be in their best interest not to. Not because it was bad or good or because we would be condemned, but because He knew it would make life much more difficult.

Eating the fruit of this tree makes living from the heart impossible because it introduces duality, which drains away life. Duality introduces the opposites of such qualities as beauty, love, joy, and light. Suddenly there are negative comparisons: not enough, better than, worse than, or just plain bad. Our day-to-day life then begins to reflect the effects of those disempowering words instead of the words that support life.

The story also tells us that there was another tree in the Garden: the Tree of Life. The Tree of Life represents the essence of life: hope, love, joy, peace, laughter, and contentment. These are qualities that enhance life and nourish our spirit. These words have meanings that cannot be measured or compared. This is the tree that God would like us to eat from.

The opposite of life is death. With death, I think of words such as, anger, fear, depression, sadness, pain, and guilt: emotions that kill our spirit and keep us from experiencing all that life has to offer. Again, this is what the Tree of the Knowledge of Good and Evil represents. The metaphor is about death. Adam and Eve were warned not to eat from this tree because death keeps our heart from dancing and destroys the energy we need for a fulfilling existence. Life gives us energy and makes our heart dance.

Good and evil are forms of duality. Duality is right versus wrong, good versus bad, and acceptable versus not acceptable. This duality creates judgment. Judging what is good and what is bad about ourselves and others kills our spirit and deadens our soul. This separates us from what we want the most, which is life and all of its essence. The story of the Garden shows us what happens when we choose judgment and duality over acceptance and love. We separate ourselves from the Divine and so from the essence of life itself. It throws us into separation, thus limiting our capacity for life and love. God doesn't want us to be limited.

The more judgment we carry, the less beauty or life can be expressed in our world. Judgments are the basis of all crusades. When we want everyone to believe as we believe because we "know" we are right, we immediately take a side and make the other side wrong. Then on some level we are at war. This philosophy has destroyed more lives than we would like to admit. God warned us not to eat of the Tree of Knowledge because it causes pain and suffering. Its fruit takes us out of our heart, where we find oneness and unity, and into our head, which tends toward duality and separation. We face this challenge every day as we can decide whether or not to walk in love or in separation. This dictates whether we stay in or walk outside of the Garden. Metaphorically, God has to protect the Tree of Life from our judgments, so if we choose to eat from the Tree of Good and Evil, we automatically take ourselves out of the Garden. Since judgment kills life, it cannot exist on the same plane as life.

Whenever we jump out of our heart and into our head, we lose the beauty and magic in each moment to duality. We are separated from the Garden because we separate ourselves from God, the Divine source of life. And by judging ourselves and others, we hide from the Great I AM, just as Adam and Eve did when God came to look for them.

In the New Testament, the word "sin" often means to separate from God or to miss the mark. It is not the act of doing something bad, as many people believe. Sin is the act of hiding from God because of what we are ashamed of in ourselves. So when Jesus said, "Go and sin no more," I don't believe he was telling us not to mess up again. I believe he was telling us not to be ashamed of who we are. He knew that we are human and messing up is how we develop mastery. It is only through our experience that we can become like God and be free of fear, shame, and guilt.

Separating from our heavenly Father keeps us from life in abundance. I was once told that God could not look upon me because I was bad and a sinner. I now understand that He can't look upon me if I'm hiding. That is all sin is: hiding from God. It never meant that I was bad.

My children have taught me a lot about this. There are moments in my life when my kids drive me crazy. At these times, I look at them with my limiting mind and can only see their shortcomings and what they are not. I am looking at them through the eyes of the Tree of Knowledge. Then there are times when I see my children through my heart, as I believe God sees us. I witness these beautiful beacons of light with infinite possibilities and great potential, and see only their perfection and goodness. Did my kids change from one moment to the next? No. Only the lens through which I was looking at them changed.

God always sees us through the heart because God is love. He doesn't see life through a filter of duality because there is no life in duality and God is life. He doesn't see us as separate or not enough. No matter where we are in our lives and how we are conducting our existence, God only sees our infinite potential as a Divine representation of His beauty, His oneness, and His creation. We were made in His image. And what a magnificent image that is!

Chapter 4

The Three Loves

Once when Jesus was asked what we needed to do to follow God, he said, "Love the Lord our God with all your heart, with all your soul, with all your mind, and with all your strength. And love your neighbor as yourself."

God is love, and the key to living life through our heart is finding a balance between the three types of love Jesus mentioned: love of God, love of others, and love of self.

I have discovered that when I can live and nurture all three loves in a balanced way, I don't have to worry about anything else. All of life falls into place easily and abundantly. If any of these loves are missing or out of balance, the flow of life through my heart is reduced and the living waters of infinity are affected. Moreover, it takes more energy to offer love to others if I am not in balance. When I have love for myself, the work I do for others flows more effortlessly and costs me so much less than when I don't. Before I found love for myself, the love I gave to others exhausted me.

Love of self was the love that was missing for my mother and me for a long time. Without this love, the other loves are not as powerful or as authentic. Like my mother and many other people who were around me when I was growing up, I was stronger in my love of God and my love of others. This is why being of service put me into such bondage. It turned what I most wanted to do into a struggle.

It is also one of the reasons my mother's beauty turned to sadness and resentment. Lack of self-love depleted her of life. If love of self is missing, it's impossible to fill your cup before or after serving others, so serving others becomes harder and harder. The living waters of life are unable to replenish your heart and soul. My mother was able to give encouraging words to everyone else, but not to herself. As time went on, her well of love became drier and drier, which pinched off the flow of love she could allow herself to receive from God and others. The same was true for me.

When Jesus said that he was one with God, he meant that his three loves were in perfect balance. Because of that, he had no need of rules or regulations. Being in balance with the three loves meant that he was always in right relationship with himself and his highest good, so he had no need for outside authorities to regulate his behavior or tell him how to live. This is why he drove the religious leaders of his day crazy. He had no need to follow the rules. His way of being and living was very threatening to the religious establishment, which, ironically, knew all of the prophecies and was waiting for the Messiah to come. The Messiah was right there under their noses, but they couldn't see him because they were looking through their minds, not their hearts. They themselves were not in balance with the three loves.

Keeping these loves in balance gives us freedom of choice and sovereignty over our actions. In order to love myself and see myself as God sees me—as a limitless, magnificent, powerful creator of my own world—I needed to address the voices in my head that were always telling me I was not enough. I had always tried to ignore them, but as they got louder and louder, I came to understand that they were keeping me from allowing self-love to flow. They were limiting my life, feeding me words from the Tree of Knowledge of Good and Evil that only invoked powerlessness. I had to die to my small self.

To truly die to self and come into life, we must step into our heart and see ourselves from the place of the infinite. By making choices from our heart, the sustainable and endless gifts of the spirit can flow to us. Life then begins to resemble the beautiful example that God gave us through Jesus.

I began the process of addressing the voices in my head by turning to them and speaking the positive words I know God uses to describe me. I had to consciously claim the truth of who I was. For example, if my small self told me I was worthless and had nothing to say, I would respond with, "I have a lot to say, and I am worthy of every blessing this earth holds." This caused the voices to lose their power over me and die to the new creature I was becoming. And I was becoming something very special, for I knew the truth. The truth is that I am fearlessly and wonderfully made by God. And the most beautiful part about this is that we all are, without exception. We have all been created with Divine purpose in the beautiful oneness of spirit. We are all linked together in love, yet we each have our own unique purpose for being in this world.

If we are able to die to self, we are better able to see ourselves as God sees us: through our heart instead of through our mind. Then we can love ourselves and open to the fullness of life that being in balance with the three loves brings. To die to self liberates us from being a victim. We are no longer ruled by our fears and worries; we no longer believe we are worthless sinners who are powerless to change our lives for the better. And we no longer feel dependent on God to create the world we want to live in. We don't have to wait for God to do it for us according to an arbitrary set of rules. God has given us the capacity to be our own creator, a creator of all that is good and edifying. We each have a unique touch—a touch that is divinely ours and reflects our individual passions and talents.

The Bible says, "Whatever is good, whatever is right, whatever brings peace; dwell on these things." This is what can be found in our heart when it is in balance with the three loves and we are not limiting ourselves with rules. The mind loves rules, and it is when we live in our head that we step out of the Garden and into duality, separating ourselves from the oneness that is God. When love of self gets too far out of reach, the mind takes over and we are unable to see or reach our full potential. Our passions and our desires grow weak, and we become old and lifeless before our time.

The head is powerless to change anything on its own, for it is rarely in present time. In our head we are always planning for the next moment and protecting ourselves from what might happen in the future, based on what we think happened in the past. In doing this, we are unable to access the magic and possibility of the moment we are in. When we live from our head, we stay busy making lists of all the rules and all the shoulds and should nots that our head tells us we need to live by instead of trusting the intuition of the moment.

It is the intuitive knowing that comes from our heart that serves us the best. The head can only base its information on our judgments, and as we have seen, these judgments limit the Great I AM in us by limiting our choices and our ability to experience freely and joyfully. It is only through choice, experience, and love that a relationship with God can be deepened. These elements take us out of separation and duality and return us to the Garden where nothing can corrupt our love.

Embracing Diversity

In the Book of Micah, God says that all He requires of us is "to do justice, love mercy, and to walk humbly before Him."

What does it mean to be humble? I think in order to be truly humble we have to know how important and how magnificent we are as we acknowledge the whole universe and everything in it. We have been created in God's image—the image of the Great I AM—and this image is not only in us but in everything around us. God has created everything so everything is God. If we truly understand this, each of us will be able to say "I AM" with confidence and humility. Each of us has great purpose in being here.

In the New Testament, when Jesus was asked how we should live our lives, he said different things to different people. To some he said, "Love God, your neighbor, and yourself." To others it was, "Believe in the one He sent." And to another, Jesus said, "Sell everything you have." This illustrates that God's word is alive and breathing and that the message is different for each person in every new moment. Each moment brings a precise message forward, for no two moments in history are exactly the same. Just as there are no two people who are exactly the same.

I feel that many things in the Bible were said in a certain way to a certain group because that group needed to hear it put in a particular context. The messages are based on where those people were in their life and the uniqueness of that moment. I don't think God intended for us to take the Bible at a literal level like it is a rulebook. That is why He installed the message of life within each of our hearts. Each of us has our own unique message that is living and breathing and changing as each new moment dictates. We only need to go within to find it. Jesus said, "The Kingdom of God is within you."

Raising my children really helped me grasp this concept. As an example, I encouraged one of my sons to be more pliable when working with others because he was too rigid. Conversely, I encouraged his brother to stand strong in his beliefs because he needed to learn to stand up for himself. To tell the child who is not pliable to stand strong might not serve him well. And to tell the one that doesn't stand up for himself to be more pliable might not serve him either.

God honors diversity; He created it in every aspect of life. So it makes no sense that He would create one set of hard and fast rules to apply to everyone. He speaks differently to each of us. The only thing He speaks of collectively is love. There will never be a perfect religion where everyone lives the same way before God. His word is alive and breathes into each and every one of us a new and different message, one that can change in the moment. He asks each one of us to walk our own unique path freely and without judging ourselves and others. Doing this creates great diversity. When we give ourselves the freedom to do this, we can allow others to walk down a path that might look nothing like ours and give them our full support. When we have freedom to choose, we can allow others the same freedom.

So in order to receive all of the power and love that God says I am capable of having, I have to love my neighbor as myself. And to do that I need to love and honor the diversity in life that God created. Then I can see the beauty in every person I meet without losing sight of my own magnificence. I can see everyone as an important part of the whole no matter what car they drive, how they were raised, what their sexual preference is, what their belief system looks like, or how they view God. When I'm able to do this, I feel I'm able to source from the true Christ energy.

God honors everyone for the choices they make. Loving the diversity of humanity and your neighbor as yourself is what makes a family, a tribe, and a community strong. All opinions count, knowing there is no one right way of doing anything. I think God had this in mind when He asked us to love our enemies as well as our neighbors. If we could truly love our enemies and see that their views have worth, this world would be a much better place.

An example that illustrates the value of embracing diversity can be seen in the Pawnee Indian tribe. Within this tribe was a group called the Crazy Dogs, who were considered very sacred. The Crazy Dogs had a special calling: the Great Mystery charged them with doing everything opposite to the rest of the tribe. If the tribe was attacked, everyone would jump and prepare for battle except for the Crazy Dogs. They would continue doing whatever they were doing before the attack occurred. If the tribe was told not to go into the water because it was too high, the Crazy Dogs would dive in. If the tribe was told to clean up, the Crazy Dogs might choose to clean up with mud instead of soap. Their role was to remind the tribe that everything is relative and that there are many ways to look at a situation. No one is necessarily wrong, nor is anyone necessarily right. The Crazy Dogs are a reminder that polar opposites can both be right, and that the truth is often found somewhere in-between. Wouldn't it be wonderful if our governments shared this perspective?

To walk in the spirit means to honor everyone's choices. We must trust ourselves and each other to make the choices that serve us the best. The process of honoring and allowing space for all ultimately brings all participants closer to their soul calling. It allows everyone to be empowered so that we can truly step into being a creator in the most conscious and powerful way. If we don't allow ourselves to choose, we get stuck and become limited in our thinking, and then we begin to limit others. If we limit diversity in our own life, we can't tolerate it in others.

None of us can truly capture the full essence of God on our own, so we need diversity to strengthen our understanding. And because no single belief can come to a full understanding of the Divine, there is no one that is absolutely right. I believe that is one of the messages Jesus was trying to show us. In John 14:6, Jesus says, "I am the way, and the truth, and the life. No one comes to the Father but by me." What I think he meant is that to really know God you must know Him the way Jesus knew Him, live life the way Jesus did, and follow your own truths the way Jesus did. Jesus knew God totally through his heart. His love did not separate, nor was his love based on following a single belief system. Jesus wasn't concerned about how others might see him. He was very comfortable being in the presence of people who appeared to have widely different beliefs than his own, and he never made them uncomfortable because of those differences. For that reason, many people sought him out. These were often people who the religious elite belittled and wouldn't associate with. Yet they didn't need to change or hide who they were in Jesus' presence. They were accepted by him, and felt completely embraced and loved.

I often wonder who would best represent this group in the world today—those that religious society will not embrace. The closest subculture that comes to mind is the gay and lesbian community. I see Jesus embracing them and allowing them their choices without any lectures. He would view them as God does in all their great potential, uniqueness, and beauty. That is what I love most about Jesus. He told us that all we need to worry about is loving the Lord our God with all our heart, mind, and strength, and loving our neighbor as we love ourselves. In other words, the three loves. If we follow this one command, everything else will fall into place.

Another story that illustrates the importance of embracing diversity without judgment and allowing self-love to grow is the story of Judas. He was the apostle known for betraying Jesus, which led to both of their deaths. It's interesting that Jesus had to pretty much kick Judas out of the Last Supper so that he would go and do what he had to do, which was to betray Christ. Before he left, Jesus gave Judas a kiss, essentially sending him on his way. Judas was also being oppressed by three demons that were pushing him into the betrayal. It's clear that Judas had a very important role to play, and that he was struggling to step up in order to perform it. It's also clear that he could not carry out his role alone; he needed Divine help.

After Jesus was crucified, Judas tried to return the money he had been paid for Jesus' capture to the religious leaders who had given it to him. They refused to take it; the money was thrown back to Judas as blood money. Finally, Judas hung himself because he couldn't forgive himself for betraying Jesus. He hung himself for something that God and Jesus had already forgiven him for; he was an important part of the plan. This was very sad indeed.

The Book of Romans talks about the fact that we are the clay and God is the potter and that God makes us all for different uses. Judas had one of the toughest roles to play in Jesus' life; perhaps in all of history. It's so easy for anyone that reads his story to take a side, judge him, and condemn him to death. I feel, however, that I'm going to see this most amazing man in Paradise, and I'm very grateful to him for showing me what can happen if we don't have self-forgiveness and self-love. I know that God forgave Judas because God forgives all; that is the whole point of Jesus' life. The problem was that Judas could not forgive himself, and because of that took his own life. He stayed in the limitations of his head, unable to see beyond the right and wrong of what he had done. He remained outside of the Garden. He was only able to allow himself a very conditional love, and because of that he quite literally limited his own life. He had the same choice we all do: forgive yourself and know that God has already forgiven you, or judge yourself and end all life.

Our world is what we have chosen to make it, whether we are consciously aware of this or not. We are powerful creators, made in the image of God, the Great Mystery Himself. We are not helpless wanderers on this planet, as we might like to think at times. We have free choice and are very capable of mastering all that we need to learn from our experiences. And we can become more and more like the Great I AM if we are willing to die to self.

If we choose not to master life's experiences, we will come to the end of our time on earth and find that all the life force inside of us is gone. We become old, and I'm not referring to the natural aging process that happens to all of us. I mean the kind of aging that happens on the inside. Whether or not we age in this way is completely up to us. Being old on the inside reflects dryness in every area of our existence and kills the life force that gives us hope. Our experiences and choices play an important role in helping us find and allow life. Now is the time to step up, choose, and trust that the Great Mystery is as powerful as He says He is. We need to trust that He will find us and bring us safely back into the fold if we get lost.

Chapter 5

The Power of Choice

When God created us, He gave us freedom of choice. He wanted us to create our lives with the same freedom He created us. He created us in His own image so we can master all that we need to master.

The story of the Prodigal Son is a great example of how the freedom to choose and experience life from this vantage point leads us back to our heart and into the Garden. In this parable, a well-to-do father had two sons. One son always did what the father asked. The other son had a freer nature and wanted to try everything that life had to offer. Many of these offerings, however, were not in his best interest. One day, this son approached his father and asked for his share of the inheritance so he could venture out and do all he desired to do. His father understood that this was what his son needed to do in order to find his heart. So he not only allowed him to go, but he gave him all he asked for in the way of money and possessions.

The boy squandered his inheritance on things that didn't last, like "sex, drugs, and rock and roll." He was trying to fill the void in his life with things that didn't serve him particularly well. Once he lost everything, he felt very alone. In order to survive, he took a remedial job with a farmer, taking care of the pigs. Even so, his job didn't provide enough, and he began to compete with the pigs for their food. It was then that he thought of how his father's servants were treated better than he was in this job. He decided to go home and beg his father for a servant's job because, having squandered so much, he couldn't possibly ask to return to his position as a son.

The surprising thing was that when his father caught sight of him, he ran out to him with open arms and embraced him as his son once again. It didn't matter that his son had squandered everything. He simply said, "My son was lost, but now he is found." He gave no lecture, no conditions, and no shaming. He wanted to celebrate his son's return, so he threw him a party and gave him his place back in the family.

The Prodigal Son's father not only allowed his son to choose, he gave him everything he needed to step out on his independent path. When his son returned, the father received the gift of his son's love. Because the son now had experience, he was able to freely choose the path that brought him life. He chose to come back to his family and was able to open his heart to their beauty and take in the goodness that had always been there. This wouldn't have been possible if he had squelched his desire to leave or if his father had forbidden it. The son followed his path of learning, which put him in situations that were not in his best interest short term. Yet in the long run he was able to master them, and so could step out of duality and back into the Garden once more.

The quality of free will is very important to God. It doesn't matter how we choose to live our lives as long as we are living them. God wants us to choose and choose freely. It's important to understand that there is a big difference between choice and consequence. There is an earthly consequence to every choice we make. Even choosing not to make a choice has a consequence. All choices have a consequence, but all of the consequences are earthly; they are not of God.

The Prodigal Son had to live with the consequences of the choices he made on his journey, such as losing all his money and fighting with pigs for food. These were the consequences of the choices he made. Would he have been able to return to his father more freely had he made better choices? We can never know. What we do know is that his choices led him back home, and he was only able to return home because of the mastery he found through the freedom he had to make these choices.

Now we can look at the oldest son and his response to his brother's homecoming. This son was out in the field doing what he felt he was supposed to do. On hearing of his brother's return and the party that was being planned in his honor, the older brother threw down his hoe and stomped off. How could his father do this for the brother who had squandered everything? He had been the diligent son, working very hard at what he felt was important, and probably ignoring many of his own desires.

What this tells us is that the older brother never allowed himself to choose freely. He justified his life through his works rather than his heart, so he couldn't step into his heart and celebrate the reuniting of his family. He couldn't allow himself to see any goodness in his brother, and so fell out of the Garden and into duality and judgment. He was stuck in his literal mind and the need to choose between right and wrong and so was unable to see the positive results of his brother's journey. His anger, hate, and envy cut him off from love, joy, forgiveness, and celebration.

Freedom to truly love can only be discovered through experience and acceptance. We can memorize the entire Bible, but the only way to be free to walk with an open heart is to experience life fully. To do this, we need to allow ourselves to have and make choices. Does this mean we have to pursue every choice there is on this earth? No, but if our freedom to choose is eliminated, our love will be limited and the Garden will be off limits.

Stepping back into the Garden is about being free to love no matter what the circumstances. Stepping back into the Garden is what the Prodigal Son was able to experience because he allowed his heart to question and pursue everything it needed to in order to come home freely and humbly. There was no mediocrity in his actions, unlike those of his older brother, who could not step outside of his self-imposed role and be joyous about the homecoming of his sibling.

For many years, I was the older brother. I tried desperately to follow all the rules that might bring me closer to the Creator I desired so much to know. The more I tried, the more rules I created for myself, and the darker my search became. I was living outside the Garden and the earthly cost had heavy consequences. I couldn't understand why it was so dark or why I felt so distant from Jesus, who said things like, "My burden is light and my yoke is easy," "Ask and you shall receive," and "The truth will set you free." Those truths weren't real to me at all. They were only words on a page, and I wasn't one to say something that I didn't believe and feel. My life felt heavy and burdensome, and there was no way I could celebrate my "younger brother's return," even though I wanted to.

So I really began to question what I was missing. I started to differentiate what I really believed in my heart from what the rest of the world told me I should believe. I set out on my own path, allowing myself choices, and as I did I felt my burdens lighten. I began to find my truth.

Ultimately, the search for my own truth led me to make one of the hardest choices I've ever had to make. I decided to leave my marriage so that I could come home to my heart and step fully back into the Garden. For 28 years I was married to a beautiful man. We raised seven children together, and were a very good team in that regard. I still love him with all my heart, but I came to realize that my love was only the love of friendship. I had fallen out of the desiring kind of love for him, and I felt trapped because I didn't want to displease God or hurt my family. Meanwhile, I resented my husband because I felt I couldn't express my true feelings about our relationship. He was very dependent on me, and will tell you now that he had walled everyone else out of his life, leaving only a small hole for God and a big hole for me. Ironically, it was much like the relationship my mother had with my father.

I tried very hard to make our relationship into the dream of what I had always wanted from a marriage. I wanted us to share a vision and work together in the world for a greater good. Because my husband was making few decisions to bring life into our family, I began to push him to do things that at least would enrich our partnership. I wanted life, but he wanted to be left alone by everyone except me. To his credit, he brought me what he thought I needed and what he hoped would bring me life, but this made him even more depleted because he wasn't choosing what served his highest good. As we got older, this problem only got bigger and more painful for both of us. I saw that we had inadvertently created rules that weren't serving either of us. We were simply doing what we thought was our duty, just like the older brother in the story of the Prodigal Son.

As I said, my marriage was becoming a lot like my parents' relationship. They had a very mother–son relationship, which could never be in balance. In the end, my mother became very demanding and controlling of my father, angrily dictating what he could and couldn't do. I did not want to end up this way, and yet to step away from my husband seemed so costly for everyone. At the same time, I wondered whose heart I was responsible for: everyone else's or my own? In answer, I heard the verse that has been my motto for many years call out, "Keep thy heart with all diligence, for out of it are the issues of life." And so, for my own life's sake, I stepped out of my marriage.

I knew this was going to create shockwaves for everyone, especially because others had often told me they wanted to have a marriage like mine. There wasn't any drama to blame my decision on. My husband and I got along quite well, but my heart was clearly calling me in another direction. I told God I would only step into my truth if He promised to take care of my husband and seven kids. I never dreamed how well He would do that, and after our separation, my husband began to step into life in a way he had not done for many years.

I had many choices as to how to go through this separation, and I chose to go through it with an open heart. Because of that, I created no extra drama and was able to stay in the Garden. My husband, my kids, and many others threw a lot of emotions at me, but I knew I had to keep my heart open if I wanted to continue to find God within. I found that the emotions coming at me were only the projections and reflections of whoever was throwing them my way.

As I stepped into my truth, I began to feel God's Divine light in a way I had never felt before. At times my head said, "You're crazy—all your security is in this marriage." But my heart said, "Thank you for honoring yourself." Now I see that my real security lies in my heart. That's where I access God's magical power, which is the power of each and every new moment. Now I know that my choice to leave has been a gift: not only to me, but also to my family and friends.

When you are in your heart, you no longer make your choices driven by the fears of yesterday or the worries of tomorrow. You realize with this magical understanding that you have everything you need, and life becomes a beautiful synchronistic dance. Since our separation, my husband—whom I am still very close to—has told me that even though he has difficulty dealing with his emotions at times, he would rather be here in this new, redefined family of ours than back in the days where he felt lifeless. And me? I'm finding out who I really am and what brings me life and passion. The passion I am speaking of is eternal.

I chose to stay in the Garden and find God's love in my heart. I didn't separate or hide from the Divine as I walked away from my marriage, and I'm so grateful for all the beauty it has brought to all the life around me. I want my children to be free to access all the beauty they can in their lives. Freeing myself up helps them discover their own freedom of choice. Their father's choice to step back into life also gives them hope for the future.

If you want your children to heal and have all that the Garden has to offer, the greatest thing you can do for them is to step toward whatever is calling your heart forward, whether others think it is for your highest good or not. If you do this, you will surely find your way back into the Garden, pursuing your own healing and feeling God's eternal love and support. And your healing will trickle down into the lives of everyone that you love.

Choice and Creation

Life is an interesting dance with many twists, turns, and choices. The freedom to choose is one of the most important gifts God gave us and depicts how we were created in His image. I gave myself the freedom to choose a different path than that of my husband, and this allowed many new creations to evolve. The freedom to choose gives us great ability to create, and creating from the heart is one of the finest things life has to offer. When we give ourselves the gift of choice and pure creation, we no longer see ourselves as trapped or as victims.

We are made in God's image, and so we are creators of our world. There isn't one moment of the day that we are not creating. Every thought we have affects the world around us; collectively these thoughts mold together to form our surroundings. Some of the thoughts are conscious; others are unconscious. But conscious or not, our thoughts blossom into the journey we have chosen to be ours. We are not innocent bystanders to life's twists and turns. We are active participants. Our beliefs and thoughts about life are reflected in the life around us for us to see and learn from.

If we see life as hard and full of sacrifice, then we'll have to work hard and sacrifice to attain the things we truly want. Although this choice might be rewarding, it also makes living a struggle, and at some point this struggle may lead to feeling worn out. Eventually, we may have to give up because we have expended so much energy on things that didn't nourish or sustain us. Then we might become angry with others or the Great I AM, and blame them for our hardship and exhaustion. The reason we blame them is because we refuse to take responsibility for the creation of our life journey.

On the other hand, if we step into our heart and listen to our soul's song, we find that no matter what life brings, we never lose sight of life's infinite possibilities. We discover that life is not about sacrifice at all. Instead, we find that life is full of choices that can bring sustainable energy and that we can build a world brimming with beauty. If we view life as full of goodness and mercy, it will be. If we view life as difficult, difficulty will make up our path of learning. If we learn life's lessons with ease, we will walk through life with ease. The choice is up to us!

I was told growing up that God creates our world and the circumstances in it and that we really can't affect those circumstances. Yet from where I stand now, I can see that we have many choices about how we lead our lives. God leaves it up to us to choose, as he did with the Prodigal Son. If we remain conscious of our choices, we can have a great effect upon our world. Our society has gone to sleep in many ways because we've been taught that we don't have the ability to affect our lives. We have lost the awareness of our ability to choose and have become victims to the unconscious choices that so rarely feed our soul. We create the world around us through our unconscious choices. This is haphazard at best, and leads us to believe we are victims in life rather than the creators of it.

Our unconscious choices often provide us with the wakeup call we need to find our way back home. The Prodigal Son fell victim to his unconscious choices after he spent his inheritance. As a result, he found himself feeding swine and eating their food. It was then that he woke up and realized he had another option. He had a choice about how he was going to live the rest of his life. This enabled him to move in a direction that ultimately served him better. The most beautiful aspect of this story is how his father received him upon his return, saying, "You are my son and will always be. You made your choices, and because of that, you now have returned to me freely and I can only receive you as my son." The freedom and love his son received in returning was worth all the wealth he once had.

The son still had a couple of choices at this point. He could accept the grace his father offered or turn it down. His father's gift was far beyond anything the son could fathom for himself. To receive it, the son had to be willing to accept his father's love and forgive himself. He could also have chosen to stay in his guilt and shame and never enter his father's house as a son again, saying he didn't deserve it or wasn't worthy, allowing himself only to be a servant. Limiting the endless possibilities that life was offering him because of the choices he made in the past.

The father in this parable is like the God I have come to know and serve. He realizes the importance of experience, and puts no blame on us for our actions. He knows that we have already felt the earthly consequences of our actions, and that there is no need to punish us.

God doesn't try to change our minds or force us into anything. He always offers us the grace of life in ever-increasing abundance. He allows us to live in whatever way we choose, knowing we will learn what we need to learn through life's trials. Hopefully, this process will show us how amazingly unique and divinely special we are. Whether we get it here on earth or later is up to us. If we are open, we will come to know how much God loves us exactly as we are.

This is the righteousness that Jesus spoke of in the New Testament. It isn't something to be attained or made into a goal. It is the righteousness we already have. It isn't based on getting our life in order and living a certain way. It exists whether we accept it or not. In the way that God is always present for us, His righteousness is always present. We don't have to follow any rules in order to attain this gift. It's our choice: we can allow it into our life or we can say, "I'm not good enough to accept this gift," or, "Until I get my life straightened out, I can't allow myself to partake in this blessing." And hence we hide from that righteousness just like Adam and Eve hid from God. God always views us as worthy of His grace. It's only when we think we aren't good enough that we step out of love and into separation.

Being righteous means to stand before God as we are, and to have faith that we are loved exactly as we are. "As we are" means that when we accept our choices, we have no regret or shame about them. God has given us the ability to create our own world, and that is what He wants most for us to do. The Great Mystery wants us to find the key to the Garden once again and return to it with an open heart. We can do this by understanding the rich metaphors of the Adam and Eve story. The main emphasis of the story is not about eating the apple; it's about separating from God. God knew that life would be easier if Adam and Eve didn't eat the apple, but He honored their choice to do so. He knew that once they ate from the Tree of Knowledge of Good and Evil and stepped into duality, humanity's freedom could only come through the journey of choice and experience.

If we don't allow ourselves to pursue experiences in life, we will never be free to come back to God and rest in who we truly are. Without experience, there are many things we cannot know. Unless we experience darkness, we can't understand light. Unless we experience sickness, we can't fully appreciate the feeling of wellness. We cannot know who we really are or fully see who He is until we experience life's choices.

Many of us limit our freedom because we are enslaved by fear and allow it to control our actions. It was such a wonderful thing for me to break out of the bondage of fear and into the freedom of choice. The only way I could do this was by allowing myself to explore the desires I had previously suppressed. I had to allow myself to experience as the Prodigal Son had allowed himself to experience. Once I began experiencing, a beautiful thing happened: I became free to step into the presence of God. All of the feelings that had held my heart in bondage, such as fear, guilt, and shame, dropped away. I was free to be me. And the most beautiful discovery is that the "me" I am becoming is more and more like the Christ of the New Testament.

This is what I was trying to be all along. But now I don't have to try anymore; I can just be. I now know that there are no right or wrong paths. Some might serve us better than others, but all paths will lead us to freedom if we allow them to. As we give ourselves the freedom to choose, God honors all of us for the choices we make.

Chapter 6

Law and the Written Word

As I stated in the preface, I wrote this book because I wanted to share the journey of my liberation from religious dogma into freedom and love. For a long time, I was bound by the outmoded and contradictory rules set down in the Bible. These rules didn't come from the conviction of my soul; they were things I was told I had to follow to gain God's love and acceptance. Most of them—especially the ones in the Old Testament—are confusing, and apply to a time when religious and state law were one and the same. Many aren't even vaguely relevant to our present time and circumstances.

As I learned to live from my heart and step back into the Garden, the dogma that led me to feel separate from God faded from my life. For a while, though, I questioned the validity and wisdom of any person or group that even attempted to write down the word of God. To me it seemed that the more it was written down, the less helpful it became. It felt like an idol I was being told to follow blindly rather than Divine inspiration.

I thought about how many spiritual traditions chose to pass down their teachings orally, and that even in the face of persecution these teachings have been protected and exist today. I even questioned whether or not I should write this book. I worried that in doing so, my words would also be held in time and lose their true message. So often we write things down because we don't trust ourselves. The ego wants to change mystery into certainty. When we allow our ego to gain control, we rob ourselves of the magic that we are all capable of possessing when we trust in God's Divine mystery. It is mystery that truly represents the Divine.

Eventually I realized that there are many pearls of wisdom among the outdated rules in the Bible. And when they are read as metaphor and viewed through the lens of the heart instead of the mind, they become the living, breathing word of God once again. They still have the power to create beautiful epiphanies that are exactly right for each new moment. The reader gets to choose how to come into relationship with them.

One reason Jesus came to earth was to nullify our belief that the Bible was intended to be taken literally and understood as law. He wanted us to view it as inspiration for living a life centered in the heart, and encouraged us to grow beyond our dependence on the written word. If, like him, we are able to live from the integrity of our heart, we will always make choices for the highest and best good for all. But until we are able to master this way of being, it's helpful to develop a conscious relationship with the written word, coming from a place of choice and free will rather than enslavement and control.

On their own, words have no power: it is how we choose to be in relationship with them that is relevant and gives them energy to empower or enslave. We decide whether certain words resonate for us or not. We can allow them to help us travel deeper into our hearts or prevent them from drawing us into our heads. We can keep a law because it's in alignment with our heart and personal integrity or break it because it doesn't work for us. We don't even need to follow the Ten Commandments literally if our heart tells us to relate to them in a different way. They are simply a set of ethical guidelines. All indigenous cultures have a version of them.

The written word is important because it's one way we communicate; it's a way to share diversity and pass on information about our world. But we choose how we relate and respond to what we read. And we can still love and be loved by God when we choose to follow our own heart path instead of an arbitrary set of recorded rules. God prefers that we take good care of ourselves, even if it means breaking some rules. He supports free will and choice. Following the written word literally, even if it is His word, really means we are hiding from God and denying ourselves the chance to step back into the Garden and to live life through our heart and without judgment.

God's message is constantly changing because our needs change. This is one problem I see with taking the written word of God as literal law. A message written yesterday might not be important today, although yesterday it was vital and alive and very relevant. But the main problem when spiritual truths are written down and become law is that we forget to listen to our heart, where God resides. God speaks to us through our heart and knows exactly what each of us needs to bring us life. He didn't intend for us to conform to laws that were directed toward someone else at a specific time for a specific reason. We can never have true freedom of choice, which is how God wants us to live, if we are bound by ancient rules of religion. And which rules should we believe? All religious sects believe that their way is the right way. Written laws can be contradictory and confusing; it's impossible for any one of them to be right.

Each of us stands before God, living how we feel is right before the Great I AM. And because we each have our own faith, God speaks differently to each of us. Our journeys are all very different, as are the maps our hearts ask us to follow. As Jesus said, "The Kingdom of God is within you." God's true power isn't easy to access if we take the Bible too literally and try to understand it with our heads. The written word becomes limiting and disempowering when we try to follow it to the letter. We need to be in a living, breathing relationship with all that God says, written and unwritten.

A friend of mine once commented that if the church fell or was proven wrong, many people would fall and lose their way. This baffled me at the time, yet I knew there was truth in what she said. I was raised with the belief that we are in a personal relationship with God through Jesus. If this is true, then we ought to know God intimately and have our own unique relationship with Him. This kind of relationship is not based on facts. Intimate relationships are of the heart, whereas facts are of the head. But so many people base their life and power on the written word instead of trying to develop a direct relationship with the Great I AM. The Bible was never intended to be a rulebook.

I have found that it is possible and desirable to relate to the Bible in a way that inspires the heart to know our own truth. Spiritual writing is only useful when it helps us remember and know God in our hearts. Our belief cannot be sustained by written words, and we will always fall short of its laws. First and foremost, we must keep our heart alive and open to the direct word of God. If we don't, the written word becomes a dry, obsolete, empty substitute for true wisdom. It makes us feel that we are never enough, and nurtures fear, guilt, and shame instead of love.

Guilt and shame are not of God. Our head will always crave more knowledge to attempt to fill the emptiness that is created by not listening to our heart. Knowledge cannot even begin to grasp the vastness of the Great Mystery; only our heart can do this. God says knowledge only puffs up our ego and brings imbalance. His way makes no sense in the literal world because we can't see the bigger Divine picture. Life is so much more than what we experience on this earthly plane.

Many people seem to revere the Bible more than they do God. Both their worldly and their spiritual security are based on how much they "know" about it. This limits their ability to love. They feel that they can only be in relationship with those who share their beliefs; they don't know how to honor someone who sees life and God differently. As they separate themselves from the greater world, their personal world shrinks. The more rules they have, the more separated they become. Anything that is not of their world feels threatening to them, so they vilify it and consider it to be "not of God." Their safety and security are based upon an external agreement rather than an internal, heart-based reference, so doctrine and law become more important than their relationships with others. This is nothing like the example Jesus set for us.

The Old Testament is full of rules. They fill our head so full of dos and don'ts that our heart gets totally lost. Then the journey toward God becomes one of trying to follow all the rules so He might look favorably upon us. The more rules we try to follow, the less we feel able to walk next to the Great I AM. Rules prevent us from stepping into our power and manifesting a unique relationship with God.

There is no doctrine more important than love. This message was reinforced for us through the life of the Christ. When unconditional love drives our choices and our actions, we can't go wrong and we don't need laws to live by. Jesus was such a beautiful example of how living in our hearts in the present moment allows us to find the love and beauty in everyone and everything. He didn't follow all the written laws, and his friends were not of great repute. This never seemed to concern him. He didn't worry about his reputation. He followed his heart wherever it led him, never letting the chatter of the written law influence his actions, trusting fully in the magic of each new moment. And because of that, Jesus found life and gave life wherever he went.

Since I have stepped more fully into my own heart and have come into a different relationship with the written laws I grew up with, I find that I am now laughing and smiling from a very deep place. Jesus was a master of this way of living; his joy overflowed. When we are living from our heart, it doesn't matter what is going on in the world around us: nothing can take that beauty and love away. We took away Jesus' physical life in the most horrible way, yet we couldn't take the love out of his heart because, as Paul said about love, "Against such there is no law." There isn't a law out there that can control love. Real love is free from all boundaries and limitations.

Jesus also said, "It is written on our hearts." The truth that sets us free is written on our hearts! The problem is that if we don't trust our heart to lead us with love, or if we don't trust love because we feel we have been betrayed, then our head takes over. When this happens, we only place trust in what we can see written down on paper. We follow those that have gone before us. We gain no mastery this way, nor do we give ourselves the opportunity to recover from past betrayals.

For me, the only way truth can be lost is if we limit it in our own life. God's truth will always be, because God is love and there are no limitations in love.

The only way to keep the limitless knowledge of the truth is to view all things through the vastness of the heart. This allows us to sense what God is telling us in the moment, understanding that with each new moment the truth needed might change. In the heart there is no right or wrong; there is only truth. Truth is understood through choice and experience, as illustrated in the story of the Prodigal Son. If we allow choice and experience to teach us, we will find ourselves back in the Garden of our heart, living in oneness with creation. Then life flows limitlessly to us and from us.

I have a good friend who keeps me up to date with what Mary, the mother of Jesus, says when she makes her miraculous appearances around the world. What I find most enjoyable and interesting about Mary's words is that they are always simple truths. "God is love," "Love yourself," and "Your heart holds the key," are all examples. Mary's statements are never big or complex. Why? Because she speaks from the heart to the heart. This is what I find so often about universal truth: it is always simple.

Perceiving the Bible as law means we spend our lives trying to live by others' interpretations. We end up adding more and more rules to the list until it's impossible to know how they can ever be followed. That's when life becomes a burden. But as our ability to view life through our heart grows, we come to know how freeing truth is. There is an infinite quality inherent in truth that sets us free. If we find that a truth is limiting us instead of setting us free, it might not be our truth at all. We could be in our head trying to live according to someone else's views. We need only go to our heart to retrieve our personal power and freedom.

God wants us to walk through life in complete love and self-sovereignty, in service to Him rather than written law. Religious authorities feel threatened when they see a person with a deep personal connection with God based on their own truth. If we are fully empowered and living the way Jesus did, why should we listen to them or follow along like sheep?

What happens when we attach rules to truth is that it moves

from our heart into the head. The more rules we attach, the more we limit truth's power to heal. Then fear can set in, which causes us to cling to the rules even more in the false belief they will bring us security. In our attempt to hold onto the truth, we become more enslaved to the rules. What we don't realize is that the living truth is always in our heart if we would just relax and feel it. But when a living truth becomes law, that law nullifies it and voids it of all magic.

The truth doesn't need to be written down in order to preserve it; it's like energy. It can never be created or destroyed. It just is. The truth of the heart is the kind of truth that has the power to change our life. It is sharper than any double-edged sword, cutting away what no longer serves our highest and best good. It is the most freeing thing one can ever experience; there are no boundaries to it. It brings us into oneness with all. It brings us hope, and all the spiritual gifts God promises. It can't be lost or stolen. It is timeless and an amazing healer. It dispels fear, shame, and guilt. It introduces us to our soul, bringing us love, hope, and power. As Jesus told us, "The truth will set you free."

I often find that when I share a story about my life, it changes to fit the moment. I emphasize different aspects of it depending on what I feel the listener needs to hear. It's the same story, yet the message can change dramatically. To write it down and try to hold onto all of its messages would be impossible. Each moment requires a different truth that is perfect for that time. The same thing is true of parables. Each time we read one, a different part might hold the teaching energy we need. One day we might learn from the Prodigal Son; another day from his father; and yet another time from the dutiful son. We must let our heart draw out the magic of the words and trust our heart's interpretation.

When we believe the written word is cast in stone, it loses its power to heal and edify because it freezes the moment, which quickly becomes yesterday. This is why I feel that we have lost the message God sent us through Jesus. We hold too tightly to the literal instead of connecting with the metaphor that is living in our heart. The Great Mystery is the creator of all there is; He is imputed on our heart and reveals Himself over and over again through all creation. It is truly possible to let go of the lifeless rules that have been etched on paper for centuries and find Him dwelling in our heart.

Chapter 7

The Kingdom of God is Within You

The Kingdom of God resides in our heart; this is where we find the God within us. We are healed and made whole when we can allow truth to touch the place in our heart where God and life are infinite and change is limitless. This leads to true and lasting changes.

In the Bible "being saved" means to be healed and made whole. To be healed and made whole is a much richer phrase than the literal interpretation because the word "saved" often means to be rescued. And being rescued implies that we are victims waiting for a power outside of ourselves to come to our aid, which is limiting. On the other hand, we can be healed and made whole from a place within us, which carries no limitations.

When we live by outside rules, allowing others to define our reality, our head and our heart become at odds with each other. We tend to feel split and are more likely to feel like a victim to life's influences rather than a co-creator with life. When we are following any dictate of our head that is not in alignment with our heart, we become double-minded and unstable. Our insides don't match our outsides and vice versa. Whenever we get caught in this kind of double bind, love has trouble growing and blossoming. It is difficult to trust our heart enough to come home to it and be made whole. It's also difficult to step out of victimhood and know the true meaning of "being saved" or what it feels like to have God within you.

I first became aware of this kind of split in myself when I was studying art education in college. I wanted to capture the essence of clowns, and found myself drawing and sculpting them repeatedly, often crying as I did. My professors told me clowns were trite and limiting as a subject. Yet I had a huge emotional connection with them. The feelings they stirred in me were so great that I continued to work with this powerful symbol, regardless of my professors' opinions. Something inside me knew it was a metaphor for my own life, but the reason didn't become clear until much later, when I learned that, like a clown, the person I was on the inside was very different from who I was on the outside.

On the outside I was trying to follow all the rules I had been taught and still hold onto the fruit of the spirit: love, joy, peace, patience, kindness, contentment, self-control. What I wanted most in life was to know God, to have a relationship with Him, and to live my life as Christ did. I tried very hard to be what I felt God wanted me to be. But the more I tried, the further away I felt, and the worse I felt about myself. It was a vicious circle. A clown can look happy and lighthearted on the outside even though he's feeling sad and hurt on the inside. That was me. In my attempts to please God, I was ignoring all of my true feelings and desires. I was ignoring my heart, the very place where the Kingdom of God resides, so I could find no love or acceptance for myself.

Truth in its purest form is life-changing and allows us to live freely in each new moment. A life touched by truth can't help but become lighter and easier. But letting go of the rules that keep us separate from our personal truth can be scary. To take away what we have relied on for safety and guidance causes fear and a feeling that utter chaos will take over. This is because we forget the greatness of God's grace. He has told us He would never leave us or forsake us. If we feel forsaken, it's because we have forsaken ourselves and our own passions and desires. We have forsaken our heart, where God's grace and power permanently reside. He also told us, "He who has begun a good work will perfect it." Are we not God's greatest work? Remember! We are His images.

One challenge we all face when starting out on the journey of the heart is knowing when it's God's voice speaking rather than the voice of the small self. I have found that if I am in doubt, I can resolve it by asking myself one simple question: "Is there any sacrifice involved on my part?" In other words, is my choice driven by fear, guilt, or shame? I also ask myself if I am ignoring my feelings in any way in order to say "yes" to this choice. And if I am, I ask if there are any boundaries I can put in place to release my discomfort. These questions help me hear the still small voice of the Most High.

Boundaries are necessary if we are asked to do something that could require a sacrifice of some sort. If, however, we know it is only for a certain amount of time or could be done in a way we might enjoy, setting a boundary of some type can mitigate any sacrifice. It is easy to do this by creating an "If" statement appropriate to the circumstances. By saying, "I can do this *if* X, Y, or Z is in place," it's possible to create safety and comfort for ourselves.

My personal definition of sacrifice is to give up something of myself for the sake of another person or event. For example, I might give up my own happiness for the sake of my children's happiness. For Jesus, sacrifice means "to make sacred." Jesus came to show us how to make all of life sacred.

I once went through a three-week period where I experienced many visions and prophecies. It was a very powerful time. During this time, I was shown that each step Jesus took on earth was a conscious, sacred choice on his part. He made no self-sacrifices that weakened or compromised him or his power. He freely chose every step of the way, acting in accordance with his heart's desire. It was his choice to give his life for us in the way that he did. It was his choice and his time. His time to step into his own unique calling, which no one else could do for him. It was his destiny.

Jesus showed us repeatedly how to let our hearts lead us to where we want to go. He walked in the joy of the Lord and in the unlimited depths of his heart. Finishing out his life following his highest calling, showing us that when we do the same, life is full of love, joy, and magic no matter what is happening around us.

Jesus came to this earth to show us how we can walk with God, and that the only thing that can separate us from God's love is a hardening of our own hearts. He showed us this way of walking right up to the end of his life, when he allowed himself to hang on the cross. Dying on the cross was the climax of his whole walk on earth. There was little cost to his earthly suffering because he was firmly in his Divine calling. This made it his greatest day. I hope that I can live my life according to my Divine calling, right up to my last dying day.

When I was young, my belief system was based on fear, guilt, and shame, which made for a very heavy load. Now whenever I sense my actions are coming from these emotions, I know it is not God I am following. The deeper I go into the "shoulds," the more bondage I feel, and I know bondage is not of God. Another way I can tell whether my head or my heart is speaking is when I feel guilt. God said there is no guilt in Jesus Christ. If there is no guilt, why should I run my life from that vantage point? If I am living by guilt, I am not running my life from the true I AM.

When I first realized this, I began to examine everything I did. No matter how good it appeared on the surface, if I was doing it from a place of guilt or shame I chose to stop doing it or put boundaries on it that gave me the desire to do it. For instance, I have a friend whose wife passed away and is now raising three young children on his own. I really love him and his children and help them out whenever I can. One day he asked me to watch his two-year-old on a regular basis. Although I know how hard he is working and that I have a genuine desire to help him out, I didn't want to commit to that kind of time. I struggled with guilt until I was able to put boundaries on my helping. I told him I would be there whenever he was in a bind, like when his children are sick, the babysitter doesn't show up, or he has something he needs to do and can't take the children with him. Now if he calls, I'm excited about giving my time. If I hadn't set that boundary, I would probably feel some resentment that would prevent me from entering the celebration his life and his children's lives bring to me.

On the whole, when I stopped allowing guilt and shame to drive my actions, my life began to feel freer. I began to feel like I was giving pleasure to the Creator of all there is. I also found that I was less judgmental of others, which made my life feel more like that of the Christ. It's so nice to be able to see the beauty in all. We truly are wonderfully made!

Life is a great celebration. We are all invited to attend, but most of us are missing out because we cannot see ourselves as God sees us, and have excluded ourselves from His Kingdom. We don't realize that we only need to be ourselves to enter and receive all the blessings He wants us to have. There are no dues or fees for walking in the spirit. All we need is the willingness to live according to the truth in our own heart. Does God ask us for burnt offerings of yearling calves, 1,000 rams, or 10,000 rivers of oil? Does He want the firstborn of our children to pay for the sins of our soul? No! What He wants is for us to be just, loving, merciful, and to walk humbly before Him. I have found such comfort in this. No sacrifice is required by God to enter His Kingdom or to celebrate life. The choice is mine, though, on how I want to allow it.

Space for this great celebration of life is hard to find if we are engaged in too much preparation and planning—in other words, too much self-sacrifice. These things often take us out of the moment and don't allow for choice and experience. Because the conscious mind cannot perceive all that life can bring; its capacity to create is too limited. The heart, on the other hand, is where life in abundance flows easily and effortlessly. The heart creates dreams that only Divine synchronicity can orchestrate. It brings this about in a way that the conscious mind can never fathom or plan for.

The Parable of the Wedding Feast illustrates how we can sometimes exclude ourselves from the celebration of life. The story goes like this: There was a wealthy ruler who invited all of his well-to-do peers to his wedding celebration. On the day of the party, however, none of the expected guests showed up. So he sent his servants out to invite anyone and everyone to the banquet. He insisted that they come as they were; telling them that they didn't need to change anything about their dress or appearance in order to attend. Absolutely no preparation was required for admission to this grand event. So the servants did as they were instructed and went to all the street corners, inviting everyone they came upon at random. And that night there was a great celebration.

The interesting thing about this parable is that the people who we might assume would want to be there, who had perhaps been preparing their whole lives for a party of this caliber, chose not to attend. Why? Was it because they were too busy trying to be something they were not? If so, they sacrificed all the fun and life there was to be had.

We do not have to gain admission to the Kingdom of God by performing special deeds or by looking and acting in a certain way. Jesus came to tell us that we are all righteous just as we are. He died to show us that no matter what we do, God regards us with love because He doesn't look upon sin. Even if we are behaving in a way that takes us out of the Garden and creates separation, He still sees us as whole. And if we cannot see ourselves this way, we are the ones that are disallowing His grace.

If we want to awaken the life and beauty within us, we must let go of the rules, drop down into our hearts, and allow the living waters there to change our entire being. God speaks differently to each and every one of us, and knows exactly what we need. This is why He only told Noah to build the ark and only asked Abraham to sacrifice his son. What He asks of us depends upon our growth, our desires, and our destiny. And where do we find what He is saying? In our heart.

Our growth comes as we shed all the laws we think we must live by and allow our own truth to gain strength and do its work. Following God is not a heavy burden. Jesus told us this when he said, "My burdens are light and my yoke is easy." Truth in its purest form is life-changing and allows us to live freely in each new moment. A life touched by truth cannot help but get lighter and easier. If we avoid living by another's rules and listen to our heart, God will tell us what we need to do in order to attain our abundance. Life is about choice, not sacrifice.

The Great I AM is found in all of us, yet we all have a different view of Him. Jesus came to show us that there are no universal rules. He was always breaking the religious rules of his day, but no one could condemn him because he walked in his truth with great integrity. It is our truth that sets us free, and when we walk in integrity we are free to be who we really are. When we are free, we are able to step into our heart's desires. Truth brings us to our heart and frees us to step deeper and deeper into the unlimited nature of the Great Mystery. Jesus' personal message to me was that I no longer needed to follow the rules I grew up with. Instead, I needed to find my truth and follow that. Then my whole life became a tribute to love, and my inside and my outside expressed the same feelings and desires.

The Meaning of Being One

The question of who Jesus really is has perplexed me all my life. My mother and the church I grew up in both viewed Jesus and God as one and the same. In church we gave Jesus the credit for everything that was good in our lives, and looked to him to explain everything that was not. He was God in the form of man more than he was man in the form of God. We used his name whenever we could, feeling that if we did, there would be greater blessings bestowed on us. But a deeper sense of who Jesus is continued to elude me. Who he said he was didn't line up with the things I was taught. Jesus said we could attain the beautiful life he represented for us when he came to earth, whereas all my church teachings indicated we could not step into God's likeness and live as Christ lived.

In addition, Jesus said that the Father was greater than he was. He also stated that he was the Son of God, that we can all be sons of God, and that God wants to be our Father. So why did the church make Jesus out to be God? On the other hand, Jesus also told us that he and the Father are one. I suspect that this is where we got the mistaken notion that Jesus and God are the same.

To understand more about the concept of being one, we can look at the concept of marriage. Marriage implies that "the two shall become one." The wife doesn't literally morph into her husband, nor does the husband become the wife as a result of their union. They are individuals, and yet metaphorically speaking there is a oneness created as a result of their coming together. But if either party loses themself within that oneness, then that oneness is lost; it lacks balance. Both individuals need to be present and stand in their own power in order to bring about and sustain the greater oneness. So even though Jesus and God the Father might be one, they need not be the same. It is simply their union that creates this greater oneness.

By the same token, we are also one with God. We are not the same as God, but we are one with Him. And in order to be one with God and each other, we must be strong in our own individuality. Many members make up the whole. This is how I believe God sees the world, as many members and one body. Everyone has a unique role to play in the world. There are no exceptions.

To go deeper still, we can step back into the metaphor of the Garden. It is only in the Garden that we can capture the magnitude of God's glory. When we are in the Garden and acting from love, which is our natural state there, we are part of the whole, not separate from it. The whole doesn't function well without each of its parts, without each of us participating as individuals. No one is left out for any reason at all. And when there is oneness, everyone works together for the greater good. There are no divisions that separate us from each other or from God. This is what I have learned about oneness.

Jesus was such an amazing example of oneness. He accepted and connected with practically everyone. Few felt like they had to hide from him or act differently in front of him. He embraced everyone who would allow him to, exactly as they were. Those who were unable to feel his love were the ones that had separated themselves from their heart and from the rest of the world. Some felt they had all the answers because they lived according to the rules. Since Jesus didn't follow their rules, they considered him evil. The only rule Jesus followed was love. The ones who were living in separation were trying, as I did in the past, to make themselves appear like more than they really were. They allowed themselves to be influenced by what others might say and think about them.

The religious elite couldn't allow themselves to be one with Jesus because he didn't follow their rules. Jesus didn't try to become one with them because he honored the gift of free will and their choice to be separate, just as God honored our choice to eat from the Tree of Knowledge of Good and Evil. He did get angry, however, when they took advantage of the less influential for the sake of a dollar. They claimed to live such pure lives, and yet were exploiting others. They also put all of their faith and trust in words and rules rather than in their heart. I believe they were the ones that were invited to the wedding feast but just couldn't let themselves come and celebrate life. When we separate ourselves through judgment and by upholding rules that aren't in keeping with our true heart path, we don't allow ourselves to celebrate the abundant life that is ours.

Everything we need to walk our path of eternity is within us. We can choose to look to others for direction, but following another's direction often will bring us short of all that God desires for us. We can spend too much of our lives looking to individuals or institutions for the right path. There is much wisdom and guidance to be had, but our soul's map is written within, and no two maps are alike. We don't need to be afraid to go before God by ourselves. We don't need to justify why we deserve to have Him in our hearts and our lives. We just are. That is enough. That is the message of Christ. He made certain that we have everything within us to be who we are uniquely meant to be. He wants us to know that we have all the resources we need in order to live according to our heart's desires, and to fully understand that the Kingdom of God is inside.

Jesus died on the cross to prove to us that we are truly worthy of all that God has for us to experience. This comprises all of the desires that live in our heart. Many people feel that they can never live up to what they think the Great I AM desires of them. As I grew up and began to question my own beliefs and the written doctrine of the church, I noticed that many people in the church felt unworthy before God, and this feeling only got worse as they got older. They were afraid to stand up before the Great I AM and say, "Here I am; see all of me." They had stepped out of the Garden and were hiding from God. They couldn't allow themselves to see the love and acceptance God had for them through Christ's example. They felt like they had to justify their life before Him and nothing they did seemed worthy enough. In fact, many people find it difficult to believe that God finds great favor and pleasure in them, even though He told us, "All that I have is yours."

Jesus came to prove to us that we could not kill the Divine's infinite love for us no matter how hard we try to push it away. This love will not change no matter what we do to it. We can spit on it, belittle it, hate it, try to kill it, but God's love will remain constant. It can't be snuffed out. God's heart is always open to us. For me, this is the message of Jesus the Christ.

A good example of God's forgiving nature comes through the story of the apostle Peter. Peter denied Jesus three times, even after Jesus warned him that he would do so. Imagine how Peter must have felt after he realized what he had done to someone he loved as much as he loved Jesus. Especially when he had claimed just hours before that he would fight for Jesus to the finish. And yet, when Jesus returned to life, he told the women he appeared to first, to go tell all the disciples "and Peter" that he was alive. He especially wanted Peter to know. How beautiful is that?

Peter had a number of choices about how to react to this news. He could act from his head and feel the shame and guilt brought about by his actions. Or he could drop into his heart and allow infinite forgiveness to wash any guilt away so he could celebrate the return of his Messiah. He could be angry at himself and deny himself the joy of seeing Jesus again or step into his heart where forgiveness is limitless and feel great joy in Jesus' return.

We face these same choices every day when we make mistakes before God and each other. God doesn't deny us love because we make an unfortunate choice. We deny ourselves that love by choosing to judge our choices, and by stepping into separation hiding from God and His love. God's view of Peter didn't change when Peter denied Jesus three times because He was only able to see Peter's infinite possibilities. But if Peter chose to separate himself from God, he wasn't allowing himself to see his own reflection in God's eyes.

God sent Jesus to us to prove one thing: that nothing can separate us from His love. Not even the cruelest act of violence. Jesus came to show us that even when terrible acts are perpetrated on us, we don't need to close our hearts and separate from the infinite love that is held there. The Kingdom of God is within us at all times. It is always our choice whether we allow it to fill us with love.

Chapter 8

Shine Your Light; Love Your Truth

God's truth cannot be created or destroyed. His truths lie inside each and every one of us on this planet. We do not have to go anywhere to find them, nor do we need to receive them from someone else. In fact, all we ever need to know in this life is within us and is protected by our very soul. It is imputed on our heart where the foundation of our soul's calling is laid out. This is what gives us life in great abundance and ignites our passions.

Our truth is our own. It will guide us through our journey on this earth, giving each of us our own unique walk. But when we are unable to stand in our power, acquiescing to someone else's truth, we lose ourselves and it becomes harder to find our way.

When we turn to outside influences to help us determine our truth, they can only give us their interpretation. And if we choose to follow another's truth, we will eventually lose our passion and desire because we are not living authentically.

Another way that we get lost and end up living in less love and abundance is by hiding our light. We often do this because we are afraid of the consequences of showing our unique beauty. "Let your light shine before men" and "don't hide it under a bushel." When your light is under a bushel, you can't see who you really are, and therefore can't fully live in your truth and power. You feel not understood or known by others. I hid my light under a bushel much of my life because I was under the illusion that if I shone too brightly or too much I would hurt someone's feelings. I also felt if I shone too much I would become big-headed and lose my relationship with God. So under the bushel my light went.

It is also true that when we shine we can become the target of others' projections. These projections are the unresolved feelings they have about their own inability to shine. This can be uncomfortable and misinterpreted if we don't understand what is happening. Sometimes it can be upsetting and even threatening. It took me a while to realize that when my light shines, it is possible for others to see their own reflection. But if they haven't fully recognized and claimed that aspect of themselves, they might condemn me or feel insecure. They might react with jealousy or some other negative emotion, because they have chosen to see my light as something unattainable for them.

What I have learned about many of the emotions we generally prefer not to experience is that they are only signs. They are signals that there is something within that we have not yet mastered. If I experience jealousy, for example, it's a sign that I haven't acknowledged my own unique gifts. When I do acknowledge them, I can look at someone else's gifts without stepping into comparison and separation. I am able to see my own specialness while recognizing their strengths. I don't have to lose myself in comparisons.

I found that trying to master my own jealousy without nurturing myself first was a hopeless cause. In order to overcome this, I first had to look at jealousy as neither right nor wrong. I neither judged myself nor condemned anyone else for this feeling. This allowed me to go deeper and find the awareness that brought me much healing and freedom.

If we are aware of how projection works, we can recognize our feelings of being "less than" as a call to wholeness. We can ask ourselves what part of us needs to be claimed in order to feel our own beauty and uniqueness. Then we can come into unity and oneness with all. It is only by finding beauty in our own light that we can feel oneness with each other and all of creation. I now know that when I trigger someone by shining and being all that I can be, I am giving them a gift. In that moment, they have an opportunity to see what they can master in their own life, and so shine as brightly as, or even brighter, than I.

An extreme and tragic example of the consequences that can occur if we are unaware of our projections is how we acted toward the Native Americans in the early years of the USA. In their creation stories, they were the ones who were asked to be keepers of the Garden by the Divine. They didn't have to leave the Garden as I did. I believe that they understood God through their hearts. They embraced oneness. They lived in harmony with all of creation, understanding the spiritual connection to every-thing and the relativity of right and wrong. They lived life from the heart and showed us how limited our own understanding of God was. In my view, we couldn't stand to see the reflection of our limited view of the Great I AM. Instead of seeing something we could work on and master in ourselves, we chose to nearly destroy the entire indigenous population. We were afraid of the diversity in cultures and chose to separate ourselves from them, and separation causes death.

The Old Testament story of Cain and Abel aptly illustrates the kind of relationship we had with the Native Americans. Cain and Abel were the sons of Adam and Eve. Cain, a tiller of the earth, represents the white man. Abel took care of the flocks and represents the indigenous people. Both Cain and Abel brought offerings to God. God was very happy with Abel and liked his offering very much. They enjoyed each other's company. Cain, however, was bothered by Abel's relationship with God. Losing sight of his own relationship with God, Cain stepped into comparison and separation. God noticed this and told Cain that there was something very important here that he could master. By "mastering," I feel He was saying to Cain he could find a better way of being for himself. But instead of looking at his own reflection and asking himself what that might be, Cain burned inside with jealousy and hatred. He couldn't see that Abel was reflecting back to him the light that he had yet to claim in himself. Instead of seeing what he could master in his own being, he killed his brother, just as we killed the Native Americans.

History repeats itself if we do not learn the lessons from the heart. How often do we condemn others instead of looking at ourselves? How often do we need to repeat history before we look to ourselves for the truth? Whenever we feel hate, jealousy, or anger towards others, there is something about our own life that is being reflected back to us. If we are able to drop into our hearts and view these reflections without judgment of others, or ourselves, they become great gifts. They show us clearly what we need to embrace so that we can walk more fully in the spirit of oneness and the unlimited beauty of our heart.

One of the most interesting aspects of the story of Cain and Abel is God's response to Cain. He was so gentle with him. Cain had killed his brother and yet God was willing to work with him. God told him the earthly consequences of his actions; Cain replied that they would be too hard on him; God told him He would protect him. God gave us the ability to choose and create our own lives. Along with that comes the freedom to master the lessons that only experience can teach us.

I doubt that life was easy for Cain, as the world he was creating was not very kind. This was reflected in his offspring; they also had trouble finding beauty in the lives they created. As I have discovered for myself, if we want to help our children find a better life, it's important to walk into our own healing and find that better life for ourselves. For some reason it seems easier to help someone else heal than to step up for healing ourselves. In the long run, though, I have found that true and lasting healing always begins with me. It was a wonderful surprise to see how my own healing trickled down and affected everyone I loved. When we ask God to bring about healing in our own life, we will find all that we need because our hearts will direct the journey. It truly is the greatest gift we can give our lineage—past, present, and future.

I chose to hide the God in me for a long time because I didn't want people to feel smaller than me. I wanted them to see their importance in life and that they were truly special. I thought the reflections people saw of themselves in me was a negative thing. So I hid my light and lost myself trying to protect others. It was only when I realized that I wasn't serving myself or anyone else by hiding that I really began to shine.

Jesus was the prime example of someone who reflects great light and attracts many upsets because of it. Those who had trouble with Jesus were clearly describing their own limitations when they reported the issues they had with him. This is very important to keep in mind as we trust our heart more and follow it openly in the world. We will trigger people as a result of this choice. They might even want to attack us if they don't feel worthy of their reflection in our light.

Understanding this has helped me realize that others' reactions to me aren't really about me, especially when I sense their anger. If I realize it's not about me, and that reflection is a gift, then I am able to let it all go and not separate. I don't take it personally and react by asking "What's wrong with me?" and "Why can't you see me for who I really am?" or get angry with them because they aren't treating me fairly. This understanding has made it much easier for my heart to remain open. I am able to stay out of the game of "attack or be attacked." I can stand in forgiveness of them as Jesus stood in forgiveness of us. He realized that his pure light reflected every part of us we were unwilling to claim. He knew it wasn't about him, but about our hesitance to keep our hearts open and master our own reflections. What a gift Jesus gave us by being willing to embody this example!

Being our authentic self is one of the greatest gifts we can offer the world. When we are authentic, we shine brilliantly because we show how we were created like no other person on this planet. As I have begun to shine, I've been amazed at the life it has given to me, and those around me. When we are able to keep our heart open and embrace all the reflections, true healing can take place. The more we are able to keep our hearts open, the more grace we can allow from God. The more grace we can allow, the more life we will find. And the more life we find, the more we will become what our soul desires us to be. We will become more like the Great Mystery. In this state, our yoke will be easy and our burdens light. We will find all the fruits life has to offer. And love will cost us very little because giving and receiving from the heart is unlimited.

When I was younger, loving others cost me dearly, getting heavier and heavier as I aged. Christ's message about freedom and carrying a light burden seemed so far out of reach until God showed me what was missing in my love equation: I wasn't honoring my heart and I did not love myself. I often told myself I had no value and had nothing worthy to say. The voices in me that told me these things—the ones I always tried to ignore—had grown louder with age. I didn't speak kindly to myself at all.

How could I foster love inside me when I addressed myself this way? I was burning myself out by not loving me.

So I began to search for how to love myself. Freedom from the negative voices came to me when I learned I could turn to them and speak the truth. I began to tell them things like, "I have very important things to say," and "I am very worthy; I have great purpose here."

As I spoke these truths, the voices got quieter and quieter. As they quieted down, I began to hear my heart more clearly so I could step away from the guilt and shame that those voices brought up, and better honor my own desires. Soon I began to feel more love for myself, and as I did this it became less and less costly for me to love others. As I became more balanced in my love for others and myself, I began to see what God was saying: that I am fearlessly and wonderfully made in His image for my own special purpose on this earth. And as I began to see that, I stopped losing myself in the beauty of everyone else's uniqueness.

Only then was I able to step into the oneness that so many of the indigenous people and Jesus spoke of: oneness with the Great I AM and all His creation. Love seems to flow from me so effortlessly now. I am so grateful to my loving Father because that flow of love is what I have always desired in my life, and it is costing me so little now to allow it. I am seeing, too, that my love is more like the love Jesus put out into the world, and that makes me feel very good. God wants me to shine and have all that is in my highest and best good. God wants me to find great joy, hope, and abundance. He is an awesome God, and if we allow Him, He will give us life beyond our wildest dreams.

Jesus showed us that we are each a unique temple that walks, sings, speaks, views life, and sees the Creator very differently from the next person. He installed the Kingdom of God inside of our hearts. Every human being has a soul map, and no two maps are the same by design. It is in our diversity that we complete each other, because love holds all things together in oneness.

Humanity remains strong because of our great diversity. We rely on each other's strengths and wisdom to withstand the tests of time. Only God can make opposites like diversity and oneness fit so perfectly together. God's oneness is diverse in the same way that Jesus is one with God. Jesus is his own unique being made so breathlessly close to the likeness of God because of the love he possesses. Yet he said, "My Father is greater than me." He is one with God but different. We are also all one, but very different from God and from each other.

Jesus came to show us that by taking the experience of God from the external to the internal, we can follow our own heart path and still celebrate our differences and our diversity. We don't need to look to a priest or any rulebook for our guidance. Now we can find our own truth in our heart and choose a path of direct revelation. By living in our own truth, we no longer have to live as everyone else lives to find acceptance.

So if we want to hear what God is saying, we shouldn't ask our neighbor or our priest, because they can only give us their interpretation. And even if it is quite close to our own truth, it can never be as close as a direct message from our heart, which is where God speaks. Everything we need to be able to connect to our soul map is within us. But in order to connect, we need to take some time to listen to the still small voice within our heart. I find that voice by spending regular time in meditation, but there are many ways to do this, and it's up to each of us to discover our own way of connecting.

This is important because there are many voices inside of us that want us to do many things. Most of those voices, however, are the ego's. Our ego, if we follow it, will always put us in bondage. When we are on the path of the ego, life is about getting more and doing more. If we find that we can never be or do enough, or if we constantly feel incomplete, we are listening to our ego. This is also true if we feel either better or worse than everyone else and are unable to find the balance between taking care of ourselves and others.

We cannot hear our soul if we are listening to our ego. The ego is important, but it was never meant to run the show. With the ego in charge, life will eventually stop welling up from our souls, and we will exist without passion. We will struggle to step into oneness with all creation, and struggle to feel the presence of God, who is always standing close by. When our ego has taken charge of our lives, we can only define ourselves by the label we keep on our calling cards, and we don't know who we are without them. So it's very important to find ways to quiet the mind, create space inside of us, and allow the still small voice to come forward and lead.

This can be difficult because the ego keeps us very busy. The ego will never tell us the truth of our heart. In fact, it will often tell us to act in opposition to the truth because it is invested in doing and trying. We will never be without our ego, for it serves great purpose when it is in balance. It is simply useful to notice when it is running the show and overriding our heart as we make choices. Letting the heart light our way will lead us to mastery through our experiences.

For me, the devil and an imbalanced ego are a lot alike, and since we are here to experience, we need them both to truly know God. This is because we don't know what light is until we experience the darkness, and we don't know what good is until we experience evil. I once heard someone say that to try and separate the good people from the bad people is impossible because we would have to cut right through the middle of everyone's heart. Well, God made us this way, and it is perfect.

I went to church for many years deeply afraid because of what I really believed about God. I was afraid of missing the mark in His and everyone else's eyes. The doctrine I was taught to follow left no room for the diversity that is born from personal truth. It was based on a collective agreement to keep a status quo in the external world so that we could find comfort with each other. For me, this comfort only encouraged me to stay behind my mask, because everyone had to have the same belief system and behave the same way in order to fit in. I didn't find comfort in that. The mask I wore was held on by what I call the "state of doing and trying," and that was far from comfortable. There is no rest in doing and trying, nor can you maintain peace when you're in that state.

Doing and trying are disempowering words that feed our ego and make us feel more separate from the rest of creation. God said, "I am that I AM." And this state is about being. We cannot allow ourselves to be if we are trying to conform to ideas of who God is and what He expects of us. We cannot hear our soul or know our soul map and the rightness of our unique truth if our life is based on doing and trying. It causes a never-ending cycle of not ever feeling enough.

When we are living in this state, we believe that people with different thoughts about God are separate from us. Someone always has to be right and someone always has to be wrong when we are doing and trying. This is separation at its deepest level.

When I was young my greatest desire was to know God. I spent every possible moment at church learning as much as I could. Many people informed me what my life would look like if I truly had the Great I AM in my heart. I tried so hard to live by what they said, holding up their interpretations as best I could. By the time I was in college I was utterly worn out because I was doing and trying so hard. It never was enough. I looked at my life at that point and I saw no real love and no mastery. I knew something was vastly wrong, and I became very discouraged. I was doing everything in my power to try to be the vessel of God, which is what I most wanted to be; yet without love I was nothing.

Spiritually I fell, and I fell hard. Then God began to work. The first thing He did was to start taking away all the hooks I used to hang my hat of "trying" on. Hooks like reading the Bible every day, witnessing (the verb not the noun), praying, and going to church. Each time He took one away, He would tell me I was "still" worthy. God took away all my doing and I learned to be as Christ did. I began to be exactly who I felt like being at any given time, realizing that I was okay and that I didn't have to hide how I felt or who I was from God. I now know that He wants me to come exactly as I am to His party, even if I just kicked the dog. As a result, I found true change for myself, the kind that only Spirit creates; the kind that finds rest for the soul.

As I allowed myself to be myself I felt lighter and happier. I started to be able to find the good in me, and as I did that, my insides changed and I became naturally who I was trying to be in the first place. I didn't have to try anymore; I was being me from the inside out. Now I am learning to embrace my light side and my dark side; all of me. God created both light and dark in all of us for good reason and for good purpose. I am listening to my heart and what my heart wants to be. Now love flows from my heart in bucketsful. That is what I wanted most all along, to be able to love like Christ. I am so very grateful for this gift.

Chapter 9

The Four Levels of Truth

On my journey through life so far, I have discovered four levels of truth: the literal, the emotional, the spiritual, and the infinite. We are not always conscious of all the levels of truth at once, however, and I have found that we can pride ourselves on being in truth at one level and not always be in truth on the other levels. To be congruent with our heart and fully present to the Great Mystery, it helps to have awareness of all four.

Truth at the literal level is about things that relate to our physical world; the things that we physically do or don't do. Let's say we take a cookie from our mom's kitchen counter. She asks us if we took the cookie. We answer with our truth, "Yes, I took the cookie." Or we choose to return the five-dollar bill that fell out of the pocket of the guy in front of us instead of keeping it. These types of truth affect the third-dimensional plane of physical actions.

Truth at the emotional level is very important to become aware of if we want to form deep and lasting relationships. Yet it is much easier to hide this type of truth than truth at the literal level. An example of emotional truth is when we are really mad at someone and they ask, "Are you mad at me?" If we are truthful, we say yes. If we say, "Nope, I'm not mad," in a way that belies the truth of how we really feel, we're hiding on an emotional level.

It's easy to overlook truth on an emotional level if we think we never tell a lie at the literal level. But if we are not truthful on an emotional level, it can really affect our close relationships, and cause much drama and misunderstanding. This leads to a lack of intimacy that drains any relationship of its life. Generally this occurs if we are more concerned with keeping the peace than speaking our truth. We get caught up in what might happen if we speak our truth and lose all our power in the moment. We don't speak up because we don't value ourselves enough or don't trust the outcome our truth will bring about. We forget that the truth will set us free and that not speaking the truth will put us into bondage.

Quite often we hold back our truth from those who are the most important to us, becoming angrier and angrier until we feel great separation in the relationship. At this point we may find ourselves blowing up. Then the truth comes out with no love surrounding it. When our truth isn't spoken in love, it can create a lot of drama and hurt. And after that we might say to ourselves, "I never want to cause so much pain again," and hold it in even more. If we do draw this kind of conclusion, however, we create a false story around truth and its effects. We believe that letting our emotions out is a bad thing because we created a lot of hurt feelings in doing so. What we are overlooking is that if the truth had been spoken much earlier and closer to the moment we became aware of it, it might have been delivered more gently and with love.

When we choose to keep the peace in the moment, we sometimes ignore our feelings. In reality there is probably no peace at all, because we're still anxious or angry inside. So it's only an appearance of peace. The person we are protecting may feel at peace, but we don't because we are carrying all the frustrations that come with not speaking our truth. This form of holding back causes disease and sickness in our bodies. It also indicates a fear of being vulnerable or rejected. If we can't tell those who are closest to us how much we care about them and love them, we are withholding our truth. This can cause barriers to intimacy and limit our love as well. We can be as afraid and unconscious of our positive truth as our negative truth.

Telling our truth at an emotional level brings about intimacy. The more we step away from the truth, the more separate and distant our relationships become. We cannot have a deep relationship with someone when we ignore and hide our truth. It takes us out of the Garden like Adam and Eve because we find ourselves eating from the tree of separation and judgment. When we are not in our truth and hiding, we are in separation. Whether we are protecting ourselves or another, we aren't trusting the Great Mystery to create perfect healing from the truth in the moment. We are separating ourselves from God.

I believe this is what happens in many marriages. For the sake of keeping peace someone steps away from their truth and hides it from their partner. Over the years, they begin to feel more and more distance in the relationship. Intimacy seems to be less and less available, and the closeness that was experienced at the start of the relationship diminishes because they haven't honored their truth over the years. The righteousness of the relationship is lost because neither one can stand before the other without exposing all of who they really are.

Many people who would never tell a lie on the literal level are blind to the lies they tell on an emotional plane. They tell the truth about the physical happenings in their lives but hide how they really feel in relationship to each other. This can create a loss of personal power that causes them to disconnect with even more of their feelings. Pretty soon they're entrenched in a vicious cycle that brings about frustration, anger, and depression. If we can't be our true self in relationship, it will limit our ability to feel a close heart connection. Withholding is a heavy burden and the temptation to hide it away makes it even worse. The displaced anger we project onto everyone else when we are living this way is merely a mirror of the feelings we can't honor in our own self. It indicates we are angry with ourselves for betraying the truth of our heart by not being honest. Over the years, this kind of anger becomes rage and cannot help but leak out into all our relationships.

There is a reason for every feeling we experience in life. Our feelings can help us determine what our heart is trying to tell us, and help us know when we are not listening. If we overlook and deny our feelings, we are overlooking our hearts too. Then life will slowly slip through our fingers. Our connection with others will become more and more shallow, until we find that we can only connect in superficial ways through surface levels of conversation. In order to have depth, we need to allow ourselves to feel deeply. We needn't react to these feelings, but we do need to allow them to teach us about our heart's calling so we can learn from them.

When we hold our truth back and don't allow ourselves to express it, it builds up inside of us. The more we hold it in, the less room we have for our other emotions, such as love, joy, kindness, and contentment. Life will always become stagnant when we allow ourselves less and less range of emotion, perhaps because emotion is energy in motion. Eventually, though, our subconscious will try to bring balance back to our being. It will begin to force the truth out of us whether we like it or not. This can bring about much confusion and upset if we are not aware of what is happening. For instance, the emotions that we are holding in could come out in a very ugly way in an area of our life that does not deserve it.

One of the most obvious places that we all experience this is behind the wheel of a car. Whether we have been the receiver or the giver, the force of anger that is expressed behind the wheel rarely has anything to do with the current situation we are in. It represents feelings that have not been acknowledged and honored in other areas of our life, possibly over many years, caused by many truths that were never allowed to be honored or spoken.

When my children were young, their father would come home from work and be very hard on them. As he began to evaluate the cause of his anger, he realized it wasn't the children that were making him angry. It was because he was not speaking his truth at work. His work anger had built up and was leaking out at home. He realized that if he wanted to be the father he desired to be, he had to speak his truth at work. Of course it seemed safer for him to unconsciously release his frustrations at home. But the kids were paying the toll. So he stepped into his fear and began to speak his truth where it needed to go. As he learned to do this, he was happier and became a better father.

When we wait for anger to bring our truth to the surface, and it shows up in an ugly way, we sometimes use it to justify our withholding. "See, that's why I don't acknowledge my truth, because it is so hurtful and mean." When we speak our truth to others without love it often puts everyone involved in a reactive, defensive mode. Little can be accomplished when the parties involved are in a state of separation. It's important to understand that it isn't our truth that caused all the drama, but our unwillingness to acknowledge and express it when it first came up that causes all the upset.

This was my struggle when I was younger. I was unable to honor and speak my emotional truth easily, so when it did finally push up through the depths and layers of unacknowledged feelings, it seemed to hurt rather than help. I began to feel that I had better keep silent because when I spoke, it only caused pain. The more silent I became, the more depressed I got. I had less and less room for other life-building emotions because I was so full of pain from holding in my truth.

This truth was surrounded by all the feelings I didn't allow to surface. I couldn't partake in the power that God promised me, because I didn't honor each moment's new truth by allowing it to be felt and heard in my heart. I did not see that suppressing my truth was causing my pain and depression. Nor did I realize that it is our feelings that determine our truth. As I acknowledged and released my feelings, I found that my truth became much gentler. And as this happened, my truth and my feelings were expressed in a much softer and loving way.

I learned too that when you are not in a healed state, when your truth finally surfaces, it has to push through so much pain that it becomes distorted, losing a lot of its power to heal. So for me the answer was to step up to my own healing. As I healed, my truth became clearer and I was able to present it with love to both myself and others. I realize now that feelings are neither good nor bad. But labeling and unacknowledged feelings cause much imbalance to our emotions. I began to see that all feelings come from my heart, where God resides with all His wisdom and power. Therefore, feelings were the keys to directing my journey from bondage to freedom. With this awakening, life began to change for me. As I began to express my truth, my emotions came into greater balance, and more beauty came welling up from within me.

Truth at the emotional level is a living and breathing energy, changing with every moment. Our truth in one moment may be totally different in the next. For instance, in one moment, we might not want to make love to our beloved, but in the very next moment we do. God told Abraham to sacrifice his son Isaac, yet in the next moment He held Abraham's arm and said it wasn't okay. We can't always take the truth of one moment and apply it to the next. Each moment holds its own truth and that truth can be accessed through a healing heart. Each moment holds a unique message for only that given time and space. Listening to all the emotions that come up can help direct us to the truth of each new moment.

The greatest thing we can do for ourselves is to listen to what our inner self is saying, knowing that there is a reason for every feeling we have. Then we can respond to what we hear and feel with sincerity, honesty, and love, acknowledging our truth and allowing it to be fluid without holding onto the truth of any particular moment as though it were eternal and unchanging. We must learn to allow our truth to evolve and change, the way the moments of our lives evolve and change.

The inability to feel truth on an emotional level can be caused by the stories we attach to our truth. Stories create expectation and limit possibilities. They are disempowering. They are created from our limited mind's thinking and from past scenarios. Stories are often created when we are children and our childlike logic wants to rationalize any wounding we received. They can stay with us throughout our adult life and limit our system of beliefs. For example, we might have grown up with a critical and self-absorbed mother who got angry whenever we told her the truth about our feelings. Because of this, we might find it easier to hide the truth about our feelings even as an adult. The story is, "Bad things can happen if I tell the truth." Blaming all the drama in our relationships on any expression of our truth always keeps us confined by our stories. They make us feel disempowered and keep us from developing deeper relation-ships. If we are able to let go of the story and express our truth in the moment, the truth will set us free.

Stories take away our power and don't allow possibility. They change expectancy to expectation, and allow life to be played out only in a very controlled way. Often when things don't work out the way we expect, we feel that God has forsaken us. This is how we limit Him, too.

If our emotional truth is static rather than fluid, it's usually because we are operating from a limited belief system. When our belief systems are rooted in past experience and based on the stories we have written in our heads, it limits us from ever seeing life any differently. It creates a very negative vein in our existence. And it limits how we allow God to work in our lives. Even if we feel our truth very keenly, we will be tempted to deny it if it is in opposition to a learned belief system or authority. This is why it is important to know what our stories are and where they come from. Otherwise we are tempted to ignore our true feelings in order to stay in alignment with a belief system that may or may not be true for us today.

Stories driven by fear carry with them many rules in order for them to exist. They hold us in bondage, limiting our power and God's to create a new story or outcome that lies beyond our wildest dreams. Oftentimes these stories become the foundations of our doctrine. If we hold too tightly to our doctrine, the doctrine becomes more important than our relationships. I have found that the best relationships in my life are free from any rules.

Intimacy is very important in every relationship. Intimacy cannot be achieved without truth, and truth can be lost when individual or mutually agreed-upon doctrines are rigidly in place. For intimacy to grow and thrive it requires fluid emotional truth and the freedom to speak that truth. If our emotions are healthy, they are always in motion. So our emotional truth must be free to move and change. When I am able to give my partner and myself the freedom to be in truth, the more intimacy I create and the closer I feel to them. Intimacy is a key ingredient in allowing righteousness, so we can stand in front of God and each other without hiding anything.

I have also learned that in order to have intimacy at its greatest level, we have to see how beautiful we really are, both in our shadow and our light. We have to put aside teasing and any other mental games because we play these games in order to hide ourselves, and our feelings, from each other. Games and teasing hide feelings we haven't yet acknowledged in ourselves. So if we find ourselves always teasing someone and dancing around the truth, there is some truth we haven't recognized within our own being. We are hiding from both ourselves and the person involved. I have found this awareness very helpful in my own life. When I sense I'm playing games or teasing, I go within and ask myself what I'm not acknowledging. The things I have learned about myself by doing this are fascinating.

We have to speak our truth even if we fear it will cause conflict. We have to speak it and then stand strong in our power to love. And listen well when the other person expresses their feelings, even if their feelings are in opposition to ours, because truth can evolve only if we keep our hearts open. That openness gives us the power to see the similarities in the opposition, bringing them together. Keeping your heart open to others' feelings influences your truth and deepens your understanding, giving you greater clarity. Truth is fluid. We have to be firm and at the same time flexible, which is a combination that can only be held in the spirit. Remember, the Great Mystery can make opposites like firm and flexible fit together perfectly. In the Tree of Life, there is no such thing as wrong or right. Truth is relative.

If we hold back our truth and don't speak it with love and power, intimacy will slip away from what was once a deep relationship. Oftentimes our ego will tell us, "Oh, that's no big deal; it really doesn't matter if I speak it or not." This choice may not affect the relationship much in that moment, but if it is a long-term relationship, the build-up from discounting our feelings will destroy intimacy in the end. This happens a lot in marriages. One spouse might start by hiding the finances, afraid that it will cause conflict in the relationship. Then he or she might hide hurt feelings, telling himself or herself it's no big deal. If we have to say to ourselves "It's no big deal," it has the potential to become a very big deal.

Soon this partner will feel like he or she is carrying the whole weight of the relationship because every single thing they hide is added weight to their own yoke. If they continue to choose not to look at the effects of not speaking their truth, they might start blaming their partner for what they haven't had the courage to express. Then both parties become confused and hurt by the anger that is unexpressed. This anger puts a wedge between them and begins to erode the intimacy they once had together.

Truth is the greatest gift we can give our partner. It will allow us to stand with no shame in great freedom, feeling totally known, accepted, and loved. In order to feel totally accepted we have to be known, whether it is in relation to our family, our spouse, or our friends. In my case, when my beliefs began to change, I hid them from my mom because I didn't want her to reject me. The more I hid them from her, however, the more distance I felt between us. I was giving up intimacy with my mom because I was afraid of what she might think of me if I spoke my truth to her. The worst part about it was I didn't even realize the cost of my choices. I began to resent my relationship with my mother because I felt as though she didn't know me at all. The truth was she didn't know me because I didn't let her know me.

I was at a very low point in my life when I came to this realization. A friend told me that she had done the same thing with her mother, and when she finally chose to open up and let her mom know who she really was, she was amazed at what it did for their relationship. It brought much balance to it and her mother didn't react at all in the way she had feared she would.

The story that my friend had written in her head that had so limited their relationship was nothing like the truth of what happened when my friend allowed her mother to know who she really was.

You see, we need the kind of diversity in relationships that only the truth can reveal. Indeed, if we want to live by the Tree of Life, we must present each truth and listen to its opposite, allowing all sides to be considered and honored. This, in turn, will bring about great depth. Being heard is so important in bringing about balance in relationships because it makes both parties feel like they are known. And there is no better feeling than being truly known by someone you love.

This is what happened to my mom and me. As I said, it was at a very low point in my life. Life had become too heavy, and I felt as though I was holding up everyone's expectations of me. So I called up my mom, invited her over, and proceeded to let her get to know me. It was such a beautiful and freeing day for us both. And like my friend's mom, she surprised me by responding very differently than the stories I had written in my head. To this day, I am so grateful for my mother's love. Not every relationship works out as easily as mine did with my mom. Some take much longer to become balanced. Taking the first step and exposing who we truly are, though, will prove to be the greatest gift we can give to all those we love.

Truth on a spiritual level allows us intimacy with God. This truth, like emotional truth, also changes and deepens as the moments of our life change. This truth brings freedom to the soul and allows us to feel the righteousness of God that is always there for us. This truth keeps our actions and our words congruent. An example of this might be a person like me, who really wanted to attain spirituality in life. I tried very hard to create the characteristics in myself that I considered would make me more like God. But in trying, I ignored who I really was and what I was really feeling. The lack of truth about how I felt on the inside only caused me to place more judgment on myself and others, creating more separation between me and God.

I think the person we hide spiritual truth from the most is ourselves, which keeps us separate from God. If we can't see ourselves for who we really are, it is much harder to go before God allowing Him to see us and stand in His righteousness. I noticed that my love for others was conditional because of the way I judged myself. I also saw how hypercritical my life had become, and fell into deep despair. What I wanted most was to love others as Christ had loved, and yet there I was, loving others so conditionally. My love was very limited and this made me sad. That's when the Creator came down, picked me up, and began to teach me about the state of being. I learned that in order to enter the state of being, I had to let go of the state of trying.

Our spiritual truth can vary greatly depending on our journey, and as we grow spiritually our truths at this level may change. When I was a child I was protected by the rules of my parents to keep me safe. I was fed milk, for example, as most children are, and I wasn't expected to make my own choices about things. As I grew, however, my rules and my food choices changed. I grew into knowing for myself what was good for me and what was not. I became a grown-up, and as a grown-up I am free to choose how I want to live my life and what to feed myself. We go through a similar progression with our spiritual journey.

Our truths at the spiritual level change as we grow. Problems only arise when we cling to those that were given to us in our youth and don't allow them to change and grow as we mature. If we cling to them as if they are doctrine, our innate wisdom cannot mature. We must allow ourselves to have the spiritual freedom God wants us to have in order to mature into our spiritual truth.

For me, drinking milk is a metaphor for living by others' convictions. And eating meat is about finding my own truth before God and living by my own convictions and standards in life that feel right to me in the moment, realizing that as the moments change so can my convictions. Stepping away from drinking milk and beginning to eat meat as an adult means to free ourselves from the rules of our youth, allowing each moment to dictate its own fresh new truth.

In the Bible it says, "The faith which you have, have as your own conviction. Happy is the man who does not convict himself in what he approves."

If we are still living by the spiritual truths of our youth, we might be living a lie even if we are trying to uphold something good. This is because many of these truths are not our truths to begin with. They were put on us by those responsible for our protection. We need to step away from those truths in order to find our own; the ones that resonate within us and enhance our own state of being. These truths ignite our passions from the soul level. If we can't let go of the truth from previous moments, we tend to hold onto the old as we try to create our new world. It's like putting new wine in old wineskins.

When we don't allow our truth to change and mature, we will find that we are not changing and maturing either. In order to grow, we have to step into the freedom that comes with maturity, so that we can be creators of our own world from the truth within us that is fresh and new in every moment. This truth is our own truth that the Christ said would be imputed on our hearts. As an adult, I feel I am not following any outside rules anymore, because the rules I now follow are the ones dictated by my heart.

You have everything you need to create your best journey full of life, and it's all within you. You can't look to anyone else for your own spiritual truth. If Abraham had come to me for my thoughts on his spiritual truth and told me he was being led to kill his only son, I know my response would have been, "Are you crazy? God would never tell anyone to do that." Yet that is exactly what God called Abraham to do in that moment. Thank goodness Abraham was firm in his spiritual truth and didn't ask someone like me!

An example of the truth on a spiritual level is a story in the New Testament about a rich young ruler who came to Jesus and said, "I have followed all the commandments; what must I do to inherit life eternal?" Jesus wasn't sure why he was asking him this, but essentially said, "Well, you've kept the command-ments—good—now sell everything you have and follow me." The man went away discouraged, thinking there was no way he could give up all of his possessions and wealth just to follow Jesus.

I believe this is a story about being spiritually honest with ourselves. Jesus' response helped the rich young ruler see that he might not be all that he thinks he is, or as aligned with his spiritual truth as he thought. He really came to Jesus looking for validation of how well he was keeping the law rather than for true reflection. He was hiding who he really was behind acts of spiritual obedience. In telling this rich man to give up all he owned and follow him, Jesus showed the man the wall he was hiding behind. With this reflection, he could find his spiritual truth if he chose to. So this story is not about us having to sell all we have in order to follow God. That is the literal translation. The metaphor is about being spiritually truthful. Honesty is what God wants most from us. The rich young ruler needs to be honored for giving Jesus his truth, which was, "No, I cannot do what you ask of me."

This man presented himself as though he knew he was all he needed to be, justifying himself with his ability to follow his interpretation of the Ten Commandments. He probably felt that when Jesus heard how well he was doing, he would receive great accolades from God. Instead of giving him praise, though, Jesus took this man to a deeper level of understanding by reflecting his real truth to him. The rich ruler must have known deep down that he was not all he was presenting himself to be. He was seeking outside approval from Jesus, who he felt was the greater man, so that he could feel justified. Jesus, sensing the separation in this man, asked him, "Why do you come to me for this that is already within you to know?" Jesus could see he was trying to be more than he really was. Jesus brought him to the understanding that he needed to listen to his own heart rather than looking to anyone else for security about his spiritual path. At the same time, he helped him realize that trying and doing don't make you right before God. It's about coming forward honestly as who you are.

There is another parable in the Bible that I think illustrates the importance of being spiritually truthful. In this instance, a father asked his two sons to work in the field for the day. The first son said, "Sure Dad, I'll get right on it." But by the end of the day, he hadn't left the couch. The second son said, "No Dad, I don't want to work in the fields today." But as the day progressed, he changed his mind and got busy working.

This parable tells me you can't know what a person's relationship is with the Divine based on their words. Those who appear to have no relationship with God may indeed have one that affects them very deeply. But if on the surface their words and convictions look nothing like how we think a spiritual person should look or behave, we discount them. Yet they could be the ones who hear the voice of their heart and follow it to their truth. The second young man's honest words might not match up with what we deem as God-fearing. Yet he is the one who gets the job done. He spoke the truth of the moment to his father. But this truth shifted as the day wore on, and he acted upon the new truth when it felt right. As it turned out, he was in alignment with his father's request after all.

His brother, however, had his words properly placed on the outside, but they didn't coincide with his actions. He obviously gave more than he wanted to give. He said he would help his father and then behaved in exactly the opposite way. He wanted his father's approval, but he wasn't being honest with himself and listening to his heart. Clearly he didn't want to work because he lounged about all day, but he went along with the request just to please his father and ignored his own truth.

When we want the approval of the Great I AM more than we want honesty, we learn to say what we think is the proper response rather than our truth. You can't stand in the power God has for you when you're not spiritually congruent with your heart. When it comes down to it, the brother who spoke the truth about how he felt is the one that I would trust. To truly find rest in the righteousness that is always there, you have to be honest with both yourself and God.

God has asked me to trust Him many times in my life and my first response has so often been, "I cannot." I remember once when my husband and I were going to see my parents. I was driving and we had the whole family in the car. My husband was telling me something about him and his friend. The feeling I was getting was that they both were being quite arrogant, separating themselves from everyone else. So I, being the good wife, proceeded to tell him my concerns about how they viewed themselves; something I had often tried to do. He looked at me and said, "I can't tell you anything," then rolled over and went to sleep.

It really bothered me that my husband felt like he couldn't tell me anything. Then I heard God speak. He said, "Kim, do you trust Me?" and I said, "Yes Lord, I trust You." He replied, "Then let *Me* change your husband." I told Him I couldn't trust Him to do that.

What I find amazing about this is that after my truthful response I actually began to trust God to change my husband. I no longer felt I had to change him myself. Telling God my truth set me free to allow my husband and God to work out their own relationship. After that, my husband began to confide in me more because he felt less and less judged by me. That always seemed so crazy to me: I tell God I can't trust Him, and in doing so, I step into a whole new level of trust.

This experience also showed me firsthand that the primary ingredient in causing change for the better is love and acceptance. We are conditioned to think that guilt and judgment will get the job done, and tend to spend a lot of time pointing out how we feel a person needs to change in order to become acceptable. If having someone judge us and point out our shortcomings is all it takes for change to occur, this would certainly be a perfect world. Jesus said that he had no guilt in him. Guilt only causes more chains of bondage, and there is no power in bondage. When we live as Christ, we are set free. We are free from doing and trying, we are free to be, and that makes us very free indeed. To me that is the "I AM" story.

Thank goodness I no longer think it's my job to tell people how to live their life. I'd rather tell them that whatever they choose, just don't separate from God. If we stand in the righteousness that Jesus died to show us, it will bring about true and beautiful changes in our life in a freeing loving way. And if the choices we are making aren't serving us, through our ability to experience we will find that out and then freely choose another path. Ask God to help and He will reveal a new path to you, one that may be beyond what you could ever ask for or think up.

Love and acceptance are what cause true and real change. These changes come from the inside, and show up on the outside later on as we align. Life will become what we dreamed it to be, full of love, joy, and freedom. I have found the choices are always mine to make. Jesus is always standing at the door knocking; it is our responsibility to open it. If we let him in, he will offer us the nourishment we need to heal our wounds. He will teach us to stand in the presence of the Great Mystery without shame, where all is perfect. Jesus came to help us see that the Great Mystery knows we are Divine, and whether we accept it or not, He will not judge us. We get so caught up in trying and doing that we miss the gift that is already ours. Jesus came to exemplify that gift, being the example of what it looks like to have more life, and life in abundance.

When we look at the truth on the infinite level, we find that it never changes. Like Great Spirit, the Great I AM, the Great Creator, the Great Mystery, and all the other names God is known by, this truth is the same yesterday, today, tomorrow, and forever. This type of truth can never be lost or stolen from us. It's universal. It's constant. For me, some of the universal truths at the infinite level are: we were made in God's image as creators; we are here to experience and have the freedom to choose our life's path; we are all one; and we are righteous before God. But the most important truth of all is: God is love. There are no laws that can influence love. And in His love there is nothing to worry about; everything will fall into place.

Jesus said God imputes Divine truth on each of our hearts. We don't need a book to keep a record of it. This truth will always take us to our purest form of innocent love. We can access this truth more clearly when our truths at all four levels are congruent. The more congruency we have at all levels, the less we will feel separated from God, and the more we will feel in oneness with all creation, infinitely loved by both ourselves and the Great Mystery. Because of this love, others will feel safe with us. We will find ourselves in more intimate relationships, not only with those who are close to us, but with everyone we encounter. When we are in this space, we have great power: power to heal, power to believe in ourselves, and power to love.

Chapter 10

Building a Foundation on Rock

A strong foundation for life is built from self-assurance, love of self, mastery of fear, and a deeply felt understanding that God dwells within us. This is what Jesus came to earth to show us. If we do not have this basis for life in place, then we're like the man in the Bible who built his house on sand instead of rock. In this parable, when the rains came—as they always do in the literal and the metaphorical—the house built on rock stood firm, whereas the house built on sand crumbled and fell.

When I was young, a house built on rock simply meant putting my faith in Jesus. This is what I learned in church. As an adult, however, having a foundation built upon the idea of Christ alone doesn't appear to be enough. Nor is it what this parable is really about.

If our house is built upon the rock of strong self-worth and the knowledge that the Kingdom of God dwells within us, then the external rains that fall on us can't affect our self-esteem or our faith in God. But if our house is built on the sands of external security, where our validation comes from outside of us, then our faith and self-esteem in everything from our work to our relationships will wash away when the rains come and make us feel like we have no foundation at all.

I have a friend who would say her house is built on Jesus the Rock. This friend has realized, however, that her feeling of worthiness is actually based on whether or not her partner finds her desirable. So if her partner is busy focusing on something else and doesn't constantly reinforce the feeling that she is desirable, her sense of self-worth crumbles. Her foundation really isn't very strong. When the rains of questioning and self-doubt come to visit, her house caves in; every storm that sweeps through tosses her about. When this is the case, we are unable to hold onto our power. We have no firm foundation in ourselves.

To create a foundation on rock, we need to follow the examples Jesus gave us rather than simply claim him as our rock and adhere to the rules of our belief system. We need to emulate how he lived and walked upon the earth in order to create a firm foundation for ourselves. Jesus knew who he was and knew his greatness before God. He saw himself as worthy and understood that he was made in the image of the Great I AM. He saw himself as a son of God. This is the example we are to follow. When he told us to love the Lord our God with all our heart and to love our neighbor as ourselves, he knew we would have all we needed to follow the Great Mystery. If our love is in balance and we follow Christ's example, we will always know what is right for ourselves. Our house will withstand the floods of time, no matter what changes come into our lives, because the foundation within us will hold firm.

Christ walked this earth in confidence and on a path of direct revelation. He received direction directly from source and didn't need to gain approval for his actions in any other way. He walked in his convictions and didn't question himself when those convictions conflicted with popular beliefs. He was a rule-breaker in the most positive sense. He knew the difference between the rules we create in order to appear good in front of others and the truth that frees us to simply be without trying.

The friend who is struggling with her self-worth in relationship to her desirability is rebuilding her foundation. She is taking the first steps in the process of becoming. She realizes that she is looking outside of her self for her worth. Our feelings of desirability and security can only be built from within. Our worth is already guaranteed; we don't need any outside validation. We are righteous. We have all we need inside of us, ready to uncover and recognize at any time. We are all born sacred and worthy. We have nothing to prove, and if we follow Jesus' example, we need never look outside of ourselves for our worth again.

Being a child of God and having a house built on rock is never about trying; it's about being. I find the state of trying is a powerless place. It feels a lot like a collapsing house. Trying sets us up for more trying. Building your house on sand means you constantly have to rebuild, so you are constantly trying.

The words we choose to use have a very powerful influence on our life and can show us what our foundation is built on. When I hear myself saying "I am trying," I find I am not standing in my true convictions. It feels like I'm in a place where the winds and waves can push me right over. Even the idea of trying makes me feel like a victim, as though I am incapable of accomplishing something no matter what. Whenever I am being, however, I am capable, strong, and firm in my convictions. I am in my "I AM" place of truth and power.

One of the ways we can determine if our house is built on sand is to notice every time we make reference to the fact that we are trying. When we say we are trying, it means there is something in our life we are not being authentic about and that we are basing our worth on whether or not we successfully achieve whatever thing our trying refers to. When we say we are trying, we are affirming the negative and saying to ourselves that there is a strong possibility we're not going to succeed. And we do not honor the mastery we have achieved already. Trying makes us feel like we will never achieve mastery.

If we notice that we use the word "trying" in a particular area, we need to stop and change the phrase "I am trying" to "I am..." Notice how that makes you feel. I always sense more power coming from within me when I take away the word "trying." I enter into a more present state. I have a lot more strength when I exchange those two phrases. It's as if I step away from being lukewarm and uncommitted into the hot or cold of choice and truth. I can feel my inner strength building the more I practice this; strength that gives me the feeling of presence and mastery.

This is a very special time in the history of our universe. The power available to us is unlike anything we have ever experienced before. It is truly an amazing time to be alive. This power, which is the internal power of love and the heart rather than the external power of discipline and dominance, can be accessed by simply stepping out of trying and into the I AM presence. I believe that the time we are living in now is what Jesus spoke of when he said we will be able to do greater things than he ever did on this earth. More than any other time in history, we have the opportunity and the momentum to step into the great shift in our universe. We can experience the power of the Great Mystery as it moves through us like never before. The choice is ours as to how we move into this new time. We can step into it trying to be present or choosing to be present.

The reason that this time is bringing up such great upheaval is because so many of us built our houses on sand, thinking it was rock. We might have some rocks in our foundation, but when the rains come, the rocks shift because we mixed them with sand. We humans often want the freedom Spirit offers us, but are reluctant to change in order to truly receive it. This is because change brings uncertainty and discomfort. So we compromise and weaken our foundation.

Uncertainty is a great tool for exposing foundations built on sand. If we are caught in indecision, afraid to change, and allow fear to run our life and create our belief systems, our foundation is built on sand. God is calling us to rethink all that we have learned about Him and all we are afraid of in regards to Him, re-evaluating any belief systems we have created to protect these fears. Fear is not of God. We must find His power within, so that regardless of what difficulties we might face, our house will stand firm. A house built on rock is a life built on a foundation of mastered fears, self-assuredness, love of one's self, and knowing that God dwells within our hearts.

The rains that fall in our life represent experiences. We know that God wants us to have a life full of experiences, because all experience serves us if we allow it to. When we build our house on sand we are not allowing the greatest version of ourselves to unfold. To know what our foundation is made of we need to pay attention to what happens to us when the rain in our life comes. This will help us see what our foundation is built of, and where it is we can rebuild to find mastery. How well do we trust and believe in ourselves when life's storms blow through?

Foundations built on rock allow rest and peace during times of stormy tribulation. They will not move, for they are built on our truth. The rock represents the infinite, immovable heart: our authentic selves. It is the rock of eternal infinite love, which knows what to do at all times, which is the God within us. Foundations built on the external world, or sand, are built on expectations and fears; everything has to be a certain way in order for them to stand. As long as the expectations are held up and the fears are not faced, the foundation feels secure. But as soon as expectations are not met and fears are acknowledged, those with a sandy foundation question everything about themselves and crumble to the ground, not knowing who they are. If we find our foundation crumbling during the storms, know that it truly is a gift. Even if our security falls apart, we can still be thankful, for this shows us where we need to rebuild on rock.

One of the most common "sandy" premises we build on is doing. If we are in this group, we only feel worthy if we're getting something done. When "doers" stop and do nothing or stop and do something pleasurable, they often feel worthless. Society has decreed that our worth depends on what we do, so this is a challenging thing to step out of. It gives us the feeling of security. Of course it is only the illusion of security; in order to keep that feeling of worth, we have to keep accomplishing more. This often prevents us from stepping into stillness before the Great I AM. The mind fills with all the things we should be doing and so we cannot stay present with God.

I have found that if I am trapped in doing and not free to be still, I have trouble hearing what God is saying to me. It is only through stillness, and listening to our heart and what it desires in relation to the highest and best good of all, that our beautiful soul map can reveal itself to us. The journey to our soul gets murky if we can't take time out to simply be and listen. The messages of our heart can best be accessed in the stillness of non-doing.

When we are trapped in a cycle of endless doing, it leaves little time for replenishing. This kind of life is not sustainable. Our days are ruled by doing and the time it takes to accomplish our tasks. If we stop doing, it feels like the ground gives way beneath us and leaves us nothing to hold onto. Our foundation is based on perpetual motion, and like the sand in an hourglass, disappears when we stop our activities. Time sifts away and takes all joy and pleasure with it.

The need to do goes deep in our society and causes us to live sacrificial lives. We tend to feel worthy only when we are sacrificing ourselves, and somehow we get convinced that this makes life better. This belief goes back many generations. It is handed down from parent to child over and over again. God has said to me many times, "I don't want your sacrifice." I truly believe He wants us to make our choices from a free place inside of our own hearts. I have found I have very limited choices when I am living in the state of self-sacrifice.

We sacrifice when we do those things our heart doesn't want to do. We do them anyway for the sake of something outside of ourselves; when we do this we are not listening to our heart and following it. We can follow our heart even if it looks wrong to every other person on earth, because we are the ones holding the map to our soul. We are the ones that know what is best for us. It wasn't until I could rest in non-doing and follow my heart that I was able to step away from sacrifice and step more fully into the freedom of choice.

I once had a series of visions where I visited all the stations of Christ. Each station represented a point where Jesus took another step toward his highest calling. God showed me this because He wanted me to see that at each of those stations Jesus had choices, and with each step he took he chose freely and without sacrifice. All the way to the cross, he was doing exactly what he desired to do.

Jesus fulfilled his heart's desire when he allowed himself to hang on the cross. He spent his life learning to trust what his heart was saying, no matter what the external world was doing. This allowed him to feel a quality of joy and pleasure that had nothing to do with how the external world cooperated with him. His joy was unconditional. It came from within his heart; it was an infinite joy that brings about a peace that passes all understanding; a peace that makes no earthly sense. And in doing so, he conquered death.

When I experienced Jesus in the Garden of Gethsemane the

night before his death, I was intrigued and comforted to see that he was afraid just like I can be. Even though he was on his highest soul-path journey, he wrestled with his choices because he sensed what the next day held. For me, the most beautiful aspect of this story is that he didn't let fear run his life. In spite of his fear, Jesus chose his greatest destiny, his highest calling, and his greatest fulfillment of joy. He knew that life was so much more than those difficult moments before and on the cross. He knew exactly who he was and why he came to earth, and that his death had great purpose. And with that he freely chose the cross. He walked next to his fears without letting them dictate his choices and stepped into his soul's highest purpose. He became the example, showing everyone that God's love can't be killed, no matter what earthly force is used against it. If you still only see sacrifice when you look at Jesus' life, you don't yet know who he really is.

If our house is built on rock we will know it, because after the floods of fear come, we will still be able to hear the still small voice of God among the voices telling us that we are not enough. Those are the voices that make us question everything we are and prevent us from hearing what our heart is truly saying. Being able and willing to listen to our heart, and then to trust it, is key to building on rock.

I discovered more about how to do this through my work with horses. Horses are amazing creatures that are able to reflect our truth to us in remarkable ways. I began working with them in a program that required me to spend long periods of time being in the herd and listening for what they might be saying to me. At first they appeared very sad. I felt deeply for them and wondered what could have made them feel that way. Then they began to speak to me, showing me in their most gentle way that it was my sadness I was feeling, not theirs. It was the sadness that I had accumulated over a lifetime of holding up and doing for everyone else. Not living by my own convictions and never feeling enough before God caused this sadness.

I was always very busy doing for everyone else. Doing for me only made me feel guilty, so I avoided it. I treated myself with great impatience, allowing the negative voices in me to tell me things I would never say to anyone else. I couldn't listen to my heart and what it was saying. My mind was under the illusion that my heart would never let me get close to God. I didn't trust my heart, so I spent a lot of time trying to justify my existence. I only felt okay if I was sacrificing my desires and myself. I spent my life denying my heart and not allowing myself to care for my own needs and wants.

This was the cause of all of my sadness. Sadness I didn't even recognize until the horses reflected it back to me. They helped me open my heart and taught me that I needed to grieve for all the moments I didn't allow my heart to lead. At first I didn't even know how to grieve. The horses showed me what I had to do. I needed to release all of the grief I carried in my soul and then allow the joy of the Lord to replace it. I find now that my greatest joy comes from allowing myself to have desires and nurturing them.

Once the horses showed me how to grieve, I had days of great sorrow, which was very hard. The wonderful thing, however, is that after the days of sorrow I would experience days filled with joy. I had never experienced joy like this before; it went so deep in me. This went on for many months. What kept me going through all the dark, sad times of grieving was the lightness and joy I experienced after each period of mourning. During the joyful moments I was truly like a calf that had been let out of the stall after a very long rest.

I am so happy to be alive during this fascinating time on our beautiful planet. I feel that through honoring my heart and allowing myself to be present to what I find there, I have found contentment. In contentment there is rest and peace for my soul.

When we live our life unable to listen to our heart, we can end up enduring our time here rather than living it, overshadowed by a heavy cloud of depression. That was my experience, and as I got older that cloud encompassed more and more of my life. I found myself merely existing, which is all I had the energy for because that cloud became so heavy. By my mid-thirties I gave up on it ever changing. I constantly prayed to be freed from this depression. But the cloud only seemed to get bigger with age.

As I mentioned in an earlier chapter, my oldest son triggered me into stepping up for the changes I needed to undertake. When he was 19 and came to me very depressed, declaring that he didn't believe that things could ever change, it was the push I needed to activate my own healing. At a soul level, things began to happen in my life. Teachers showed up and God began to ask me if I was ready to find out who I was and what He really wanted from me. He told me I was ready to find out who I really was, what I really believed, and what I really wanted, and through this I would find Him. He also said that when I was ready to see who He really was, there would be great blessings waiting for me—blessings that had always been there but I hadn't allowed myself to receive because of the way I saw Him and the way I saw myself. That is what the Divine said to me.

To build our house on rock we have to die to our old self. The old self can be all those beliefs that limit our view of the Divine. Some might be rules that served us in our youth that we no longer need as adults. To die to our old self is to die to everything that limits our understanding of God and the God within us; these views can warp our vision of ourselves. I have found that this limited understanding is usually accompanied by judgment and duality, causing us to step out of the Garden. We separate from God, each other, and from our own heart. For me this resulted in depression.

There is much talk in the Bible about dying to self. When I was young I interpreted this to mean self-sacrifice and thought that in order to die to myself I couldn't listen to my heart. Indeed, I thought my heart would lead me astray and take me far away from my soul's desire, which for me was to know God. To die to self meant ignoring my own desires and doing what my head thought was good and right for me. Often the things I did were good deeds, but the more I did, the heavier my life became. My interpretation of dying to self only fed my cloud of depression.

To escape my depression, I had to step out of the church and away from all I had been taught about God. I had to redefine what I truly believed. This was a hard decision to make because I knew many people around me wouldn't understand and would judge me harshly for it. I also had my children to raise and be responsible for, and I wanted them to know God too. But my desire to know God in a new way was stronger than my desire for others to accept and understand me, so I stepped out. And I am so grateful now that I did, as I stand here before you with joy in my heart.

I learned that I needed to honor myself and treat myself with the same respect I give others. Most of all I learned that the map to my soul, which carries everything that God has promised, resides in my heart. So I can trust what my heart is saying to me, honoring it and following its lead. As I do this, I get to know God better and become more like Him. Getting to know God can only bring change for the better in our life. The wonderful thing is there is no trying in that change. I am holding onto what Jesus said: that we will do greater things than he did. The time for these greater things is now. There is much happening on this planet, and I believe this is the time that Jesus spoke of. God is manifesting Himself in greater ways than ever before. I know He is moving in my life as I have never felt Him before.

To die to self means to die to the ego. When the ego is in charge, it inhabits our mind and issues messages of lack and "less than." This is why the mind is so limited. When the ego is out of balance, it has a ferocious appetite; one that can never be satisfied. When you try to quench it, as we all so often do, it only enslaves us to its needs. It denies us our God-given freedom—

the freedom that Jesus spoke of.

If we find that no matter what we do we still have a negative voice in our head telling us "This is not enough; you need to try harder; maybe someday you'll be okay," it's a pretty good bet that it's our ego informing us. The ego loves to deceive us and steal our authenticity and power, keeping us far away from the desires of our heart. It will enslave us into feeding all our insecurities from external sources, which only make them bigger and hungrier. Following our ego instead of our heart will never allow us to transform our insecurities into gifts. Gifts that God so wants us to have.

The ego is very adept at keeping us stuck in the sand, making sure we have to rebuild our foundation after every storm that comes by. To truly build our house on rock, our truths have to mirror our heart. These truths bring hope and acceptance to all that are around us. They also give us strength to develop the patience that brings out our kindness. They bring us into oneness with all creation, never separating us one from another. And they bring us back into the Garden. They do not make us feel smaller or better than the next person. In these truths we find we are enough, so there is no need to resort to bragging, arrogance, or jealousy. They help us feel secure in our position. We know the truth is always in our heart, so we no longer need external validation.

These truths free us to commune with all, whether they are like-minded or not. We will know what is best, not only for ourselves, but for everyone around us. The truth will bear all things, believe all things, hope all things, and endure all things. The truth brings us to wholeness and that wholeness is complete in love. In the Bible Paul says, "We can only know in part, and prophesy in part, but when the perfect comes, the partial will be done away with." What makes perfection is love. And I believe the time we are living in now is the time that Paul was speaking about. God is revealing to us all that we missed regarding what

Jesus came to teach us, and that is the depth and breadth of eternal love.

If we follow the truth and attach no stories to its outcome, the outcome will evolve in a most amazing way. It will show up in a way that we could never fathom. The problem for so many of us is that the ego wants to step in and figure out how things are going to work out. When we think back on our life, we'll find it's full of stories that our ego has fed us about the outcome of different situations, oftentimes instilling fear deep inside. This fear steals away all the joy of the present moment, and because we put so much energy into envisioning the many possible outcomes, we find little energy left for life.

The stories we write can really paralyze us with fear and keep us away from our hearts. They rob us of many of the beautiful moments in our life. I have found that it is in the present moment that God's greatest power can be accessed. And if our ego is running our life, it will keep our focus either in the past or off into the future, creating a loss of power in the moment. Our ego will have us build our life on sand, no matter how much we claim to be building on rock. If the ego is in charge, memorizing the Bible, building altars, and spending hours in prayer will not create a solid foundation. If our house is built on the idea of Jesus without dying first to self, we cannot empower our true self through our heart.

I believe we glean our foundation of rock through Jesus' example of how to live. He knew the Divine, and he also knew himself. He knew he was very special and worthy of all God's blessings; he didn't question himself. And even when those he knew turned against him, he did not waver in his mission. Nor did he base his decisions on the external world of logic and fear. He found his truth deep within his heart. So when his personal storm came—the greatest storm in history—he didn't get tossed with the wind or get driven away from his calling. His foundation was firmly built. He lived by his convictions and stood strong in them, modeling this to the world. At the same time, he was so gentle and loving that others couldn't help but walk away from him loving themselves all the more. It is self-love that causes truly lasting change.

And yet the greatest quest in life is not about knowing God and Jesus; it's about getting to know our self and to fall in love with the unique individual that we are. It's been wonderful for me to see that God created me especially for this very moment, to bring to the world something that can only be created and expressed through me. There is no other person like each of us on this planet.

If we can rest in this, I think we are on our way to building a strong and beautiful house on a foundation that will endure the test of time. Life will change, we will get old, trials will come, and no matter how difficult or how much change happens, our foundation of self-love will stand firm. Our fruits will keep multiplying, becoming fuller and riper with each passing year, with our greatest fruit coming in our final days.

Having a foundation on rock allows us to step into all the power God has for us, the power that Jesus said would enable us to do greater things than he. After all, we are created in God's image and so are very powerful beings. God's image is infinite, and His belief in what we are capable of is infinite too. Do not be afraid of that power. It is the power of love, for God is love.

"Power" can be a scary word because of the way in which it is often used in our society and the people we tend to associate it with. Here we must distinguish between ego-driven power, which is power that is used over others to control, and internal spiritual power. Hitler was an example of ego-driven power, and he hurt many people. Jesus was an example of internal spiritual power. True power does not look upon sin. It brings about oneness so there is no separation or duality, seeing the connection in all. Those who abuse their power seek to cause separation by creating fear and tyranny. True internal power doesn't look for who is greater; it sees greatness in the least of us. True power stands in its convictions. If those convictions are slapped to the ground, true power will stand and turn the other cheek, just as Jesus did, holding steady and unwavering in the truth. This type of strength does not come from this world.

Gandhi, like Jesus, was a beautiful example of this type of power. Neither man held any kind of office, yet their influence was great. They both stood strong in their power, and even when they were slapped down, they stood back up and turned the other cheek. None of this world's ego-driven power had any control over their beliefs. They did not question what God told them, even when the rest of the world disagreed. They stood strong and they stood firm for peace and love.

True power only creates goodness and mercy in its wake. If we can cultivate this power on a foundation of rock, it will fuel love within our being, bring balance to our existence, and help us weather every storm that blows through our life, causing our fruits to overflow effortlessly. This is the kind of power that comes from within and will fuel the shift that is changing our world.

Chapter 11

Trust

What does trust really mean? I have been pondering this for quite some time now and have found that, just like truth, trust has many levels. The three that seem particularly important are trust in God, trust in self, and trust in others.

Regarding trust in God, the verse that comes to mind is, "Trust in the Lord with all your heart and lean not on your own understanding; in all your ways acknowledge Him and He will direct your path."

To me, "lean not on your own understanding" means that His ways don't make logical sense to us. The world won't necessarily see our Divine direction as sensible, in part because the Divine speaks differently to everyone on this planet. So what is spoken to you might never have been said to anyone else ever before.

Only you can know what God is saying to you. No one else can tell you what your journey should be or show you what is imputed on your own heart. We are all here to allow and experience, and just as there are no two people alike, there are no two journeys alike. God's creativity is even more endless than our own. Trusting in the diverse aspects of life is something that is very important for us to experience, knowing that none of us were intended to be exactly alike. Moreover, everything is part of a greater picture. That bigger picture may not be clear to us, but it is very clear to God. The specific details may not make sense until the whole is revealed, which may or may not happen for us in this lifetime.

We often see things very differently in retrospect than in the moment. What might seem like a very difficult event to understand in our life now could become crystal clear when we have moved further on our journey and look back on it. Then we might be able to see why things had to unfold the way they did, and to see all the gifts that came as a result. The difficulties we have to navigate usually allow for great mastery and learning.

I have a friend who owns a business in a very depressed town. Two years ago, the business was getting close to closing. This friend received a vision and made some changes that brought about the revenue she needed to keep the business open. It was a magical time: the right people came into her life and everything panned out perfectly and easily. There was Divine synchronicity in all that happened. Today, however, she is facing bankruptcy and trying everything to hold the business together. She feels like she has lost her connection with the Divine because He doesn't appear to be working as logically as He did in the past. I, however, believe she is being asked to step into a deeper level of trust. Trust that comes from the heart and is not based on everything going in a logical, predictable direction. It is a trust that "leans not on your own understanding," and therefore cannot be based on logic or the notion that everything will go the way she expects it to. I believe the Great Mystery led her through her earlier experience to show her He finds favor in her. The old situation is a reminder that He is present and will direct her path; she just needs to trust in the unseen. This new path is leading her to an even deeper trust, one that is from the heart and does not waver when the storms come, one that allows her to be able to remain present in every moment and find great spiritual power if she is open to it.

The depression that I experienced for the first 40 years of my life was a teacher I didn't understand until later. When I was in it, I couldn't understand why it was there. Looking back, I am so amazed at how it assisted me in developing trust and helped me see the need for change in my life. We don't always understand the trials that come, but I believe everything we experience has a reason. God knows our heart, what we desire the most, and what will bring us the greatest fulfillment. In order for us to be free to receive our heart's deepest desire, however, there often needs to be growth and the development of trust. Iron sharpens iron. Being unable to follow my heart and the sadness it caused finally allowed me to step out, follow my heart, and trust it fully.

I have found that when God is working in my life, no matter how many scenarios I come up with or how a situation might come about, He accomplishes things in a way I could never have imagined. When God is involved, we will never be able to figure out the step-by-step process of it: in fact I dare you to try. Because I will guarantee He will work it out in a way that we could never figure out logically beforehand. Lately I have seen Him work in my life as never before and not once has it been in the manner I expected Him to. The result might have been what I expected, or better than I expected, but the manner in which it happened was unpredictable.

Not leaning on our own understanding points to our tendency to write stories from our head about outcomes. We need to state what we desire without worrying about how we will get it. Then we can watch God bring about the outcome that is for our highest and best good; each moment being an opportunity for the Creator of all things to be creative again and again. His ways are beautiful, infinite, and filled with genius.

Then we have the line, "in all your ways acknowledge Him and He will direct your path." This means that when we acknowledge Him, we can realize who He is and the power He possesses, which will lead us to see the Divine in all things. Everything that happens here on this planet in some way repeats the Divine synchronicity of God and the oneness we can all be a part of.

In my early forties, shortly after beginning a deep healing process, I experienced a kundalini awakening. This is where God sent His energy into each of my energy centers known as "chakras." This was not an easy state to hold. I had to spend much of the time lying quietly because so much energy was flowing through me. It was very challenging to my nervous system, and gave me a huge headache because I wasn't grounded enough to be able to handle all that it enabled me to see. I was in this altered state for about three weeks.

I found myself viewing life as I had never seen it before. It was as though a veil had been lifted and I was able to see the connections between everything, knowing that everything happens by Divine design. It was the most amazing time for me. I understood that there are no chance happenings or lucky breaks; all of creation is working together to bring good to us if we will open our hearts and allow it. So for me to "acknowledge Him in all my ways" is for me to see His hand in everything that happens to me and around me. There is Divine purpose in everything. I saw that He shows us the path to our soul in all creation if we choose to see it, and that He directs us perfectly along the way.

One lesson God kept showing me at that time was that there are no mistakes. You see, at this point in my life I was afraid of saying the wrong thing or doing the wrong thing, so I had decided it would be best if I just said and did as little as possible. My being was curling up in a little ball and giving up because I felt like when I did speak up or take action, it created pain for me and others, and that was the last thing I wanted.

I received such great insight during this experience that my desire to call someone and tell them about it was very strong. But no matter how hard I tried to reach someone, something got in the way. Through this God told me if it was important for that person to hear this information, I would get through. And if it was not, I wouldn't get through. He also told me to trust myself and allow myself to do and say whatever I wanted. He would protect me and whomever I tried to contact. His greatest will would always prevail. This was so freeing for me, as I had really given up and withdrawn from the world at that point in my life.

"Trust in the Lord with all your heart" means we have to have trust that the universe is on our side and not out to get us. We are co-creators of our world. If we feel that God and the universe cannot be trusted, then life will present itself that way. He will allow us to experience life in an untrusting world so that we can then master our lack of trust. He wants us to walk in our power as a whole person in freedom, and in order to do this we have to be allowed to master our life. Of course, in order to find mastery we often have to experience the opposite. In order to master trust, we have to know what it is like not to trust. I believe this is why choice is so important to God; He wants us to be able to stand in our power freely and in great knowing.

There is a oneness we feel with everything when we are divinely connected to God. The original keepers of the Garden taught us how important it is to stay connected to everything in Divine synchronicity. Many indigenous peoples understood this and followed it, hearing God's voice in everything around them. Just as the circle of life is repeated in every molecule, our path to wholeness is repeated wherever we look if we choose to see it. So we can trust in the Lord and experience Him speaking to us through all creation.

The second form of trust is trust in yourself. For me this was the most difficult form of trust to develop. I never understood why I trusted that God loved everyone else, yet I could find no rest in His love for me nor find any trust in Him. I was always afraid that God would overlook me; that I would miss the mark in some way and be lost for the rest of my life. What I eventually realized was that my struggle stemmed more from my lack of self-trust than from not trusting God. So no matter how hard I worked at trusting God, it made no difference, because that wasn't what was missing. What was missing was trust in myself.

In relationships, if one partner doesn't listen to the needs of the other, trust cannot be fostered. The same thing happens internally when we don't listen to our heart. We cannot find trust in ourselves if we don't take care of ourselves. Our heart is like a child within us and that child has needs and desires. If those needs and desires are not taken into consideration and are always overlooked in favor of taking care of others, then how can this inner child ever find trust in us? It is not just a matter of deciding to trust ourselves; it is also about taking action, listening to what that inner child needs, and doing whatever is needed to create safety for that part of us. When we listen to our heart and honor it, we can make the decision to trust ourselves completely. After that, our inside will be congruent with our outside with no trying on our part.

Our world mirrors our inner being. We are the creators of our world, and if we are not listening to our heart, creating in a way that makes us feel cared for, we will find that we are lacking in trust. My inner child often needed space and time to get comfortable with a new situation. If I didn't listen to her, I would often find myself in an uncomfortable situation. I frequently jumped in without giving myself any space to adjust, thereby ignoring my inner child and all of her discomfort. I ended up this way because I didn't want to ask too much from others; I couldn't give myself what I needed because I was always tending to what someone else needed. If I'd only given myself a little space and time to step in gradually, my heart might have felt safe and my self-trust would have grown.

Learning to trust ourselves is a matter of listening to our own feelings. When we sense our inner child is afraid, we need to stop and take note of our situation, and where in our body we are feeling uncomfortable. Every feeling we have tells us something, and we may be missing the lesson if we find that we react in a knee-jerk way when certain feelings arise.

It is better to be in a conscious relationship with our feelings than to let them unconsciously drive our reactions. For instance, when we feel anger, we can go within and ask, "Why am I angry? What can I do to assist me to feel safe enough to step away from my anger? What is this anger trying to tell me?" Our feelings are often a sign that something within us is not in balance. Our emotions hold the keys to our freedom of being; we need to read them, not react to them. There is a reason for our feelings and the reason doesn't always warrant an outward reaction. All feelings help us find the map to our soul purpose if we allow them to. It is important to keep from categorizing them as right or wrong.

When I was young I was often told that feelings don't matter and can't be trusted. "If you stick to the facts you will find God," they said. Yet the verse says, "Lean not on your own under-standing." To me, this means we have to follow our heart, not our logic, because our heart is where God resides.

If we don't honor our feelings, our feelings get more and more exaggerated as we get older and they try harder to get our attention. They're like the child in the classroom who has to go to the bathroom. He raises his hand nicely but doesn't get noticed.

Pretty soon, he ends up dancing around in his chair and making all kinds of ruckus to get the teacher's attention. And who can blame him? In my case, the consequence of not listening to my heart and the child within me was a deep depression. I listened to everyone else and followed all the literal facts that made earthly sense. It wasn't until I began to throw out all the rules others said would lead me to God that the depression began to leave. This didn't require drugs. I simply needed to honor and love my inner child and find my own set of rules; ones that made my heart and inner child feel safe and free.

It isn't that I don't live by any rules; it's that the rules I live by are based on my own convictions. They are for me and me alone. As I quoted earlier, "The faith that you have, have as your own conviction. Happy is the man who does not convict himself in what he approves." We are all on a journey and no two journeys are the same. No two sets of rules should be the same either. If we are living by outdated rules or rules that others have advised us to live by, our joy will never be complete.

If this statement makes us worry about "cheap grace," then we have just limited the power of God to work within. Grace is grace and there is no such thing as cheap grace. If there was, then grace would be something that we can attain through hard work and trying. As I have said previously, the state of trying is a powerless state and if grace is dependent upon doing something or not doing something, then it is not grace at all. Grace is always free. The father of the Prodigal Son gave freely, knowing that in order for his son to find the freedom he needed to live fully, he had to experience life in his own way. This included the cost of the lifestyle he chose. But because of that, his son willingly returned home, and the father got his son back fully present. What a gift of grace that was!

So to trust ourselves, we have to live by our own set of rules; rules that give us both freedom and power. We have to listen to our inner child and honor its feelings. Again, feelings are the map to balancing our soul so we can have congruence both inside and outside of us. We have to take responsibility for the world we have created, knowing that we can create great change and make our world beautiful because God made us creators like Himself.

And then there is trust in others. This has much to do with developing intimacy and being willing to step into our truth. It also has to do with clarity. Truth creates clarity and clarity creates intimacy. I have found that the people who know me intimately are the ones who tend not to question my motives, because they understand who I really am. They know me by my heart and don't judge me by my outside actions. So if we find we don't have trust in our life, it might have to do with how intimate we are with God, ourselves, and with others. Intimacy is being able to stand in our thoughts, beliefs, and feelings with another person or with God without feeling the need to hide or change anything. In that state of openness, we feel completely understood and accepted. We feel no need to justify because we are seen and known. We don't need to hide behind teasing or justification. We can say what we mean and mean what we say. And if the ones we are intimate with don't understand us, they can ask us questions to gain clarity without us becoming defensive or them losing sight of everything they already know about us.

We often hide our fears behind defensive walls and by justifying our feelings. I have found the best way to have more intimacy in my relationships is to speak about my fears with an open heart and allow my walls to dissolve. This means I discuss my fear without writing a story about the outcome. I also am willing to be completely honest and present with all of my feelings concerning my fear. Sometimes we need to dialogue with someone else in order to truly find freedom and understanding. We don't need to be right, and they don't need to change us; it's about communicating to gain greater clarity.

Many times in relationships, there is a hope that our partner will complete us where we feel incomplete and separate. This makes for very strong expectations. We also project obligations onto others in this way. The problem with this is that no one else can make us complete—not even God. We are the only ones that can do this. God and others can give us support, but until we choose to step into our wholeness, the insecurities that make us feel separate will always remain.

Sometimes just acknowledging our fear is all that is needed to deepen or maintain our intimacy with another; sometimes there is nothing to figure out. My very best friend and I have come a long way in this regard. When our relationship was young, we were often jealous of one other, which caused us to play some nasty games and created big walls between us. We later found, though, that if we spoke of our jealousy with honesty and without expecting the other to make it right, we no longer needed to play any games. It freed us up to love each other in a much deeper way. We discovered all we had to do was be a sacred witness to what the other was struggling with. It was so freeing to speak our truth and our fears out loud. The truth sets us free to trust others.

We being unable to see and feel our own importance in the world and the life we live cause jealousy. It causes us to lose sight of how special we are when noticing someone else's gifts. It is not something that we can force away as much as it is an indicator that we are not in balance with our own self-love. It tells us that we might not be taking care of our inner child by feeding her comforting words, seeing and acknowledging her uniqueness, and showing her love.

If we struggle with jealousy, it helps to fully acknowledge our own beauty and begin to make a list of our own good qualities. When we feel the jealousy coming on, we can remind ourselves that there is only one of us and that we are fearlessly and wonderfully made in the image of God. This way we will come to know that we have something that only we can bring to this world, just as the person triggering our jealousy does. As I have come to discover my own beauty, I have been able to see more and more talent and beauty in others without getting jealous. And if jealousy does get triggered, which happens sometimes, I know the answer lies within me, and that there is something in me I am not honoring.

Speaking our truth to get the other person to stop doing what triggers us will not get us very far in our attempt to create inner balance. I have found it best to speak my truth only for my own balance. I don't want to try to manipulate the other person into coddling my insecurities by changing their behavior. When I was a little girl I was teased because I was the tallest and heaviest in most of my grade-school classes. As I grew, I shed the pounds and came to the weight that was good for my build. But the boys still liked to tease me in high school and it would stop me in my tracks. My insecurity loomed and was in my face once again. I wanted them to stop teasing me so I could feel good about myself. No matter how much I tried to control what they said about me, it didn't fill my void of insecurity. It wasn't until I embraced my physical body as perfect exactly the way it was that I could find security within myself. I no longer had to control my outer world to protect that security. The triggers could be released because my cup was full of grace for myself. I knew that no matter what was said to me, my strength came from within and I knew who I was.

The issue is never about them changing; it is about us speaking. There is a big difference here. When I was younger and had trouble with someone, I often would go to them and tell them everything they were doing to me in the hope that they would change for my benefit. This caused a lot of drama and put the other person on the defensive. It's difficult to create balance through opposition. I was viewing the situation as them versus me. Healing cannot happen in this kind of duality. Duality only brings separation, and separation does not bring healing. Eventually I found that if I took the focus off them and made statements about how I felt instead, the relationship became more balanced and our intimacy deepened. I no longer felt like others needed to change for me, which released me from my "them-versus-me" attitude. This allowed us to work together to create a relational balance where both parties were free. Shifting the focus from "You are doing" to "I feel" let us work together for a common goal of a better relationship, thereby creating greater trust as well.

Feelings are neither wrong nor right. They just are. This realization allows us to make great strides in intimacy. I no longer feel the need to justify myself and prove that my feelings are right. It has also made me realize that the issue is not always about me, so I no longer take everything that is said to me so personally. I now know that every feeling I experience has great purpose. They are there to help me bring balance to myself in all my relationships so I can live authentically. They are like puzzle pieces. As we put them together, we begin to see the deeper picture of what needs to be balanced so we can step fully into our authentic self in every moment. So often we view our feelings as something we need to hide as if they are bad. Actually, the opposite is true: they are important signals to be honored and witnessed, neither bad nor good. We certainly can't get rid of them; that would be like taking the batteries out of a smoke detector. We create them as a way to help us know when we're out of balance in our life. They are merely signs to direct us. If we honor them, they will lead us to freedom if we allow them to. I have found that the path of healing always leads me inside of myself, because that is where the Kingdom of God is, and that is where healing is complete. Remember, when Jesus spoke of being saved, he meant, "to be healed and made whole."

So feelings are not always there to be acted upon. They are there to bring us to a deeper understanding of our self. Problems only arise when we act on our feelings without considering what they have come to help us master in our being; when we allow them to run our actions without seeking the deeper meaning behind them. If we choose not to find mastery from them, we will get caught in a vicious cycle that will never let up. There is a wonderful book called *Riding Between the Worlds*, by Linda Kohanov. In it she beautifully explains the connection between feelings and emotions, which she came to understand by working with horses. It is a good book to read if you find yourself caught in the vicious cycle with feelings.

I also found that having no preconceived agenda when speaking my truth is very powerful. So often we want to be like lawyers and have a full case to justify our feelings before we even step into our truth. We forget that feelings are feelings, neither wrong nor right. There's no need to justify them because they just are. All of God's healing happens in the sacred witnessing of the moment. To step into that moment with all our guns cocked and loaded, our case already argued and won, is to have no trust. This attitude does not allow the spirit to move freely to bring the balance that we desire with another into being. We have to let go and allow the dance to take us where it will, for in each moment the dance is influenced by the power of the Divine. As we begin to dance with another being in this way, the dynamics of the moment bring in new insights and direction. As I have said before, God's greatest power can only be accessed in the newness of every moment. So we must walk into each moment with a clean slate, knowing that all we need will unfold. This is trust.

If we don't speak our truth, we will find a wall going up between our partner and ourselves. Our partner may be a spouse, a relative, a friend, a co-worker, or a loved one. But no matter who it is, that wall becomes stronger and stronger if we honor our separation instead of our truth. Whenever I feel a wall going up between the one I am in relationship with, I consider it a cue to go and speak to that person in love. I have come to cherish intimacy, and I do not want to hold my love back from anyone. That is exactly what walls do—hold back love. I have noticed that walls get built whenever I complain to everyone else about a relationship but avoid speaking directly to the person involved. This is when intimacy begins to wane. I find though, that when I approach the one I am complaining about with my truth and an open heart, the relationship begins to be restored.

I have also come to realize that proving my point is not the way to restore intimacy either. The answer lies in knowing that both parties have feelings that are neither wrong nor right. This attitude allows for more open expression, disassembling the walls between us. Then, in great respect and honor, we can step back into the oneness of intimacy, often ending up even closer than we were before.

The wall that comes between people and creates separation is the wall Adam and Eve created in the Garden between them and God. As I have said earlier, this story is not about eating the apple; it is about separating from God and losing intimacy with Him because we hid ourselves. God never hides Himself from us. Even when we do the most horrendous things, He never turns His back. We are the ones who step away from Him. We are the ones who hide. He is the one who always waits patiently for us to come out of hiding. And if we speak our truth at that moment, it will set us free.

Intimacy and trust aren't something that just happens; they are like flowers that grow within a relationship if it is well taken care of. This requires balance in both parties. If we aren't willing to expose ourselves, then intimacy will be limited. Intimacy often starts with one person's willingness to step in deeper, let go of his or her ego, and be vulnerable and trust. This allows the other to feel safe and go deeper too.

Stepping into our truth is what brings about intimacy, and intimacy brings about trust. Our truth can sometimes be the hardest thing to speak because we create stories around it and fear what it might elicit in the other person. But if it is not spoken, both trust and intimacy—two of the most beautiful aspects of being in a relationship — will be limited. We cannot have trust without truth. We cannot have truth without intimacy. And the only way to truly step into our truth and into intimacy is by allowing our heart to lead us into each new moment, knowing that all we need is there and that God in all His power is with us.

My prayer for all who read this book is that you will find the God within and in doing so be free to trust and follow your heart. If you allow it to, it will take you on a most beautiful journey of healing and wholeness. This is truly what the world needs now.

Blessings to you all.